Law Enforcement

Other books in the Careers for the Twenty-First Century series:

Aeronautics

Medicine

The News Media

Careers
for the
Twenty-First
Century

Law
Enforcement

By Patrice Cassedy

LUCENT BOOKS
SAN DIEGO, CALIFORNIA

THOMSON

GALE

Detroit • New York • San Diego • San Francisco
Boston • New Haven, Conn. • Waterville, Maine
London • Munich

Library of Congress Cataloging-in-Publication Data

Cassedy, Patrice.
    Law enforcement / by Patrice Cassedy.
       p.   cm. — (Careers for the 21st century)
Includes bibliographical references and index.
Summary: An overview of careers in the various fields of law enforcement,
including educational requirements, salaries, necessary personality traits, job
descriptions, and the dangers inherent in some positions.
    ISBN 1-56006-899-X (hardcover : alk. paper)
    1. Law enforcement—Vocational guidance—United States—Juvenile
literature. [1. Law enforcement—Vocational guidance. 2. Vocational guidance.]
I. Title. II. Careers for the 21st century (San Diego, Calif.)
    HV7922 .C37 2002
    363.2'3'02373—dc21

                                                                2001005782

Copyright 2002 by Lucent Books,
an imprint of The Gale Group
10911 Technology Place, San Diego, CA 92127

Printed in the U.S.A.

Contents

FOREWORD   6

INTRODUCTION
An Array of Opportunities   8

CHAPTER 1
Federal Agents   11

CHAPTER 2
Correctional Officers   28

CHAPTER 3
Police Officers and Detectives   45

CHAPTER 4
Criminalists and Crime Scene Technicians   62

CHAPTER 5
Probation and Parole Officers   77

Notes   93
Organizations to Contact   98
For Further Reading   101
Works Consulted   103
Index   106
Picture Credits   112
About the Author   112

Foreword

Young people in the twenty-first century are faced with a dizzying array of possibilities for careers as they become adults. However, the advances of technology and a world economy in which events in one nation increasingly affect events in other nations have made the job market extremely competitive. Young people entering the job market today must possess a combination of technological knowledge and an understanding of the cultural and socioeconomic factors that affect the working world. Don Tapscott, internationally known author and consultant on the effects of technology in business, government, and society, supports this idea, saying, "Yes, this country needs more technology graduates, as they fuel the digital economy. But . . . we have an equally strong need for those with a broader [humanities] background who can work in tandem with technical specialists, helping create and manage the [workplace] environment." To succeed in this job market young people today must enter it with a certain amount of specialized knowledge, preparation, and practical experience. In addition, they must possess the drive to update their job skills continually to match rapidly occurring technological, economic, and social changes.

Young people entering the twenty-first-century job market must carefully research and plan the education and training they will need to work in their chosen career. High school graduates can no longer go straight into a job where they can hope to advance to positions of higher pay, better working conditions, and increased responsibility without first entering a training program, trade school, or college. For example, aircraft mechanics must attend schools that offer Federal Aviation Administration–accredited programs. These programs offer a broad-based curriculum that requires students to demonstrate an understanding of the basic principles of flight, aircraft function, and electronics. Students must also master computer technology used for diagnosing problems and show that they can apply what they learn toward routine maintenance and any number of needed repairs. With further education, an aircraft mechanic can gain increasingly specialized licenses that place him or her in the job market for positions of higher pay and greater responsibility.

In addition to technology skills, young people must understand how to communicate and work effectively with colleagues or clients from diverse backgrounds. James Billington, librarian of Congress, ascertains that "we do not have a global village, but rather a globe on which there are a whole lot of new villages . . . each trying to get its own place in the world, and anybody who's going to deal with this world is going to have to relate better to more of it." For example, flight attendants are increasingly being expected to know one or more foreign languages in order for them to better serve the needs of international passengers. Electrical engineers collaborating with a sister company in Russia on a project must be aware of cultural differences that could affect communication between the project members and, ultimately, the success of the project.

The Lucent Books Careers for the Twenty-First Century series discusses how these ideas come into play in such competitive career fields as aeronautics, biotechnology, computer technology, engineering, education, law enforcement, and medicine. Each title in the series discusses from five to seven different careers available in the respective field. The series provides a comprehensive view of what it's like to work in a particular job and what it takes to succeed in it. Each chapter encompasses a career's most recent trends in education and training, job responsibilities, the work environment and conditions, special challenges, earnings, and opportunities for advancement. Primary and secondary source quotes enliven the text. Sidebars expand on issues related to each career, including topics such as gender issues in the workplace, personal stories that demonstrate exceptional on the job experiences, and the latest technology and its potential for use in a particular career. Every volume includes an Organizations to Contact list as well as annotated bibliographies. Books in this series provide readers with pertinent information for deciding on a career, and a launching point for further research.

An Array of Opportunities

Jobs in law enforcement are so varied that niches exist for individuals with a host of different talents and interests. For example, criminalistics is a relatively small field for science graduates who wish to use their skills to analyze evidence and help solve crimes. Criminalists use a variety of intricate instruments to analyze evidence collected from the crime scenes. They and the technicians who gather this evidence share a passion for detail. However, technicians do not necessarily need science degrees. Thus, someone with less education who is motivated to work hard in the strange and often difficult

An FBI trainee learns how to subdue a suspect.

Police officers patrol a busy street.

settings in which crimes are committed can be trained to become a crime scene technician.

Individuals who have not graduated from college but who communicate well with others might consider careers in corrections. While the old stereotype of a prison guard is one who exerts control with brawn, women and men who work in corrections today are expected to use "people skills" to defuse potential conflicts and avert violence. The field of corrections is closely related to the fields of probation and parole, where college graduates in psychology or similar areas of study work with offenders released into the community. These professionals tackle two challenging roles—enforcing the conditions of the release and helping offenders adjust to a new life.

For those interested in a more immediate and traditional approach to law enforcement, working in a federal agency such as the Federal Bureau of Investigation (FBI) or as a police officer are two well-known law enforcement careers. These agents and officers prevent and investigate crimes. They may develop specialties, which evolve and are influenced by changes in the criminal fabric of America. Thus, police who have jurisdiction at a local level focus more and more energy on gang violence and drug-related crimes. At the federal level, the events of September 11, 2001, triggered a new, dominant emphasis on protecting Americans from terrorism.

All of these careers offer the opportunity for growth and career development, from mastering a new kind of microscope to unraveling the mysteries of bombs. Although these jobs are publicly funded and therefore subject to budget limitations, all offer opportunities for well-educated, motivated workers as the twenty-first century unfolds. FBI special agent Chuck Knowles sums up why these careers should be of interest to qualified young women and men: "We need good people. I'll be gone someday, and will need someone to take my place."[1]

Chapter 1

Federal Agents

Challenging and satisfying jobs exist in many federal law enforcement agencies, but two of the best-known and most sought-after positions are as special agent with the Federal Bureau of Investigation (FBI) or the Bureau of Alcohol, Tobacco, and Firearms (ATF). The FBI has the broadest crime-fighting authority of any federal agency. Its eleven thousand special agents combat, investigate, and bring to prosecution violations of over two hundred national laws ranging from copyright violations to kidnapping. The ATF's two thousand agents have a more narrow mission that includes preventing and investigating crimes such as illegal gun sales, bombings, and arson (purposely setting fires).

From Fire Wreckage to Murder Scene

As arson investigators, special agents of the ATF respond to the scene of major fires. For example, if a large apartment complex burns, local law enforcement officials ask the agency to help find out if the blaze was deliberately set and therefore a criminal act of arson. ATF agents first interview witnesses to find out where the fire started and how it spread. Next they sift through the structure's remains looking for evidence that carelessness or an accident—for instance, someone smoking in bed—caused the fire. If investigators do not find indications that a blaze was unintentional, they begin searching for signs that someone set the fire on purpose.

New York Times reporter Robert Hanley details the investigation of a large apartment fire—including the search for telltale signs of arson such as gasoline:

The [ATF] arson investigators focused their attention this afternoon on debris in the complex's southwestern corner [where residents reported the fire began]. . . . Mr. Green, of the ATF, said the arson investigators were trying to pinpoint the spot where the fire started. If they find it, he said, they

An ATF agent examines evidence in a gun-smuggling case.

will look for signs of accidental causes, like electrical malfunctions. If the investigators rule out an accidental cause, they will search for arson clues using dogs trained to detect the odors of gasoline and other accelerants.[2]

To investigate illegal gun sales, ATF agents may go undercover, posing as individuals involved in or on the fringes of criminal activity. The purpose of this dangerous work is to allow an agent to get close enough to the criminal activity to collect incriminating evidence. In one instance, ATF agents pretended they wanted to purchase illegal guns and then arrested the criminals who participated in the sale. In another case, an ATF agent posed as a member of a motorcycle gang for several months. He collected evidence that gang members committed a murder and were illegally buying guns and drugs. The undercover work led to thirty arrests.

Some FBI agents also work undercover. In a famous example, FBI agent Joseph D. Pistone worked undercover in organized crime for six years. Over one hundred people were convicted on the strength of his later testimony about illegal activities he observed firsthand. Pistone received a Distinguished Service Award from the U.S. attorney general and his life was chronicled in the 1997 feature film *Donnie Brasco*.

Other FBI agents investigate homicides (murders). Called "gun carriers" or "case agents," they respond to the scene of the crime and oversee the collection of important evidence ranging from fingerprints to personal objects a criminal may have dropped. They also develop profiles of the victim and the unknown attacker in order to discover the motivation behind the murder and narrow the search for the murderer. Special Agent Brad Garrett, who in his many years of service solved some of the bureau's most difficult cases, suggests the types of questions an agent asks in beginning to build these profiles:

> You look at where the murder occurred. Was it indoors, outdoors, in a highly populated or isolated area? Did the murderer sneak up on the victim? All those things tell you about a person. [You see] what kind of weapon was used, why certain things are in the house, what's missing, and what's out of place. You look at the victim's background. [Was he or she

FBI agents cordon off a crime scene during a murder investigation.

into] stock fraud or a spy, or whatever [might be the cause of] being killed?[3]

Informants and Paperwork

Thanks to sensational depictions of the agency in the media, a certain mystique surrounds the FBI and its investigations. But Garrett explains that the real life of an agent is often quite undramatic: "Ninety-five percent of my job is not glamorous and can be draining—including surveillance, reading reports, and trying to get the right information out of people."[4] Information gathering can be as mundane as working with federal prosecutors to subpoena records such as hotel bills that show travel destinations of a suspect. Or they can involve work with informants—individuals on the fringes of criminal activity who know details about an agent's case. Agent Chuck Knowles describes the process of convincing an informant to help: "You might [get familiar with] a guy in a restaurant who knows something. You have to take him aside and give him a sales pitch, build his confidence by suggesting that Uncle Sam needs strong people like him. The best cases are where you have several sources, but sometimes informants can be difficult to work with."[5]

A considerable amount of time is also spent on paperwork. Reports must be prepared each time a source is questioned. An agent may type a short report, but longer reports are dictated for transcription by a typing pool. Although documenting interviews can be time-consuming, preserving details can be an important part of solving a case. "For one home invader case my report was thirty pages long," explains Knowles. "But it was useful for later work to look back and see what people knew."[6] Carefully written reports can help prosecutors decide which witnesses to call or prompt new leads for the agent.

Hard Work and Danger

These many different tasks often cannot be completed in a typical workweek. Because the workload is heavy, and because criminals themselves do not work nine-to-five, agents often keep daunting hours. Garrett's typical week consists of weekdays that start at five in the morning with a two-hour workout in the gym, followed by twelve hours on the job. He takes Saturdays off and works a "short" day—eight hours—on Sunday.

An FBI agent wears a protective vest.

Working so hard can become frustrating when there is public pressure to complete an investigation in an impossibly short time. Garrett believes that media depictions of law enforcement create unrealistic expectations in those outside the field: "Despite what 'NYPD Blues' says, we don't solve cases in fifty-five minutes. People expect this and get frustrated with us right away. [It's true that] a lot of these cases get solved quickly, but a lot go on for years."[7]

The workload is not the only problem that federal agents face. Danger and controversy are realities of the job. Even with some of the best training in the world, agents can become involved in serious situations that lead to injury and even death. In some cases, those under investigation or innocent bystanders are harmed. When such incidents are publicized, agents may find themselves the subject of public controversy or end up explaining their actions in court.

A Positive Attitude

Although agents are well aware of these job negatives, the best face them head on and with positive attitudes. Knowles describes how, with experience, he has learned to keep a positive attitude about the long and irregular hours: "It's not like you can punch a clock. I've accepted and learned to deal with the fact that my pager goes off on the weekends. But it would be nice at times to tune it out and not have to think about it." Knowles also makes it clear that the FBI has room for those who want to adhere to a more regular schedule: "[Working] anything beyond [the usual hours] is up to what you have going on. [Some] agents may have more routine work [such as solving white-collar crime] that may take place in front of a computer."[8]

For ATF special agent and public information officer John D'Angelo, working fourteen-hour days, weekends, or, if the need arises, in the middle of the night just comes with the territory. And, like most agents, D'Angelo has little time to think about public controversy or potential danger on a day-to-day basis. While he acknowledges that everyone in his business is in the spotlight to a certain degree, he believes they are not preoccupied by it. Instead, they focus primarily on "putting people in jail and doing good investigations."[9] The potential for danger is also not a daily focus for Knowles, who says, "[We know it] always exists but we train to prevent accidents and to make sure we are very efficient and minimize danger to ourselves and the public."[10]

A Proud Realization of Childhood Dreams

Perhaps the reason these agents remain upbeat is that they feel part of something special, a perception that may date back to childhood. One of the first female agents, Barbara Wallace, was hooked after an FBI agent visited her sixth-grade class to talk about his work. Knowles chose his career because of a book he repeatedly looked at during third-grade trips to the library: "I would read about [former FBI director J. Edgar] Hoover and the gangsters of the twenties and thirties. In college I took an [introduction] to criminal justice class and when I graduated I knocked on the door at [an FBI] field office. I asked how I could become an agent and was told to get three years of police experience and then come back and apply."[11]

Knowles followed the advice, put in his time as a police officer, and went on to the FBI. He has not been disappointed. Reflecting on his many years of experience, he concludes, "There isn't a better job than being a case agent."[12] D'Angelo also expresses pride in the work of the ATF: "It serves an important function—maintaining peace and security within the U.S. and putting some of the most violent criminals away."[13]

This pride is based on the reputations of these agencies. The ATF and FBI are respected throughout the federal justice system, and their agents are routinely relied upon as the ultimate resource. For example, the skills of the FBI were "absolutely essential" to the

Special Agent Barbara "Bobi" Wallace

The FBI began hiring female special agents in the early 1970s. The successful career of one agent, Barbara "Bobi" Wallace, is described by journalist Carlienne Frisch in "Profiles of Four Occupations," from the Spring 1996 issue of Careers and Colleges.

Wallace's first assignment as a special agent took her to New Haven, Connecticut, where she worked on investigations involving organized crime, child pornography, narcotics, and bank robbery. . . . Wallace's background in public relations and journalism eventually led her to the Washington (DC) Metropolitan Field Office, where she was named media representative, making her the first woman to hold that position in a field office. Wallace is currently a supervisory special agent over the Drug Demand Reduction/Community Outreach program. She's on call 24 hours a day, seven days a week, and she usually works almost 60 hours per week. She spends over half her time traveling to area schools and government agencies, and the remainder of her time is spent handling paperwork in her office. She occasionally travels for speaking engagements across the country, and she must always carry a firearm.

An FBI "wanted" poster for a killer is stamped "captured." The agency puts away many violent criminals.

success of cases brought by attorney Tom Connolly when he was an assistant U.S. attorney (federal prosecutor):

> It came to the point where on virtually every case I would bring the FBI in even if it was not their original jurisdiction because of the resources they can bring to bear. The best agents were absolutely persistent, like a dog with a bone, and would not give up on a case until every lead was tracked down. Even after an arrest, the FBI works very hard at making cases [that a prosecutor can win in court]. And in court, where they are a lot, they typically make very good witnesses. They are trained [for this] at academy and in-house. They are well educated, articulate, and do a very good job on the witness stand. [They are] fundamentally patriotic and care a great deal about their communities.[14]

A Chance to Specialize and Work Independently

Individuals willing to take the initiative to be the best at what they do will find the philosophies of the ATF and FBI to their liking. D'Angelo explains that he enjoys working in the ATF for many reasons, but especially because it allows an agent to develop a chosen specialty: "If someone has a [certain] interest, they can choose a path that will allow them to do that. They could join the special response team that handles high-risk arrest warrant executions, or become an expert in identifying firearms. Beyond these special skills there is also room for a person interested in a specific type of criminal—outlaw bikers, [for example]."[15]

For Knowles, one of the most favorable aspects of his job is the sense that he is his own boss: "Working as a special agent is probably as close to being in business for yourself as you can be without having to pay rent or hire a secretary. Except for investigations that start out as a citizen complaint, no one really hands you the case." While this kind of independence translates into increased responsibility to doggedly develop informants and to follow up on leads, it also means that an agent has the freedom to structure the workday. As Knowles puts it, "I get a lot of satisfaction from knowing that someone's not looking over my shoulder. And the more results you get, the more freedom and latitude you get from management."[16]

Teamwork and Communication Skills Are Essential

With this kind of independence, agents are necessarily self-starters— they must look for cases and develop them with little supervision. As D'Angelo characterizes effectiveness on the job, "You have to be a go-getter. If there's information out there you have to know how to get it and how to use it to take criminals off the street."[17] For example, ATF agents may keep in touch with informants to find out if certain guns have become available in the area, a possible sign that agents should look into whether a ring of criminals has begun shipments.

While independence is a desired and necessary trait, the ability to work on a team is undoubtedly one of the most important components of these jobs. As D'Angelo puts it, "Agents rely on one another for support and safety. You have to get along with one another, and you have to be flexible."[18]

One of the skills of a good team player is the ability to communicate with different types of people. In the context of an agent's job, this variety is great. In one week he or she might deal with people from many walks of life and with all levels of education, from suspects to scientists to accountants to attorneys. Garrett puts it this way: "Probably the most important characteristic [for an agent] is the ability to talk to people, hear what they have to say, and evaluate what they say, asking yourself, 'Why is he saying that?' It's an ability to connect to people and figure out where they are coming

Agents arrest an accused drug dealer.

from."[19] Although agents are trained in communication skills, some people may be naturally more effective in this role. According to former prosecutor Connolly, there is a "real talent to getting suspects to talk. It takes a special skill with people."[20]

Good communication and salesmanship may make the difference between getting a case prosecuted and having it overlooked in the offices of prosecutors who are severely overworked. Knowles reports that he is constantly on the phone to prosecutors to urge them to make his cases a priority: "You have to get the prosecutor interested in your case by [keeping in touch] and explaining why they should prosecute."[21]

Other important characteristics for an agent include open-mindedness and an ability to distinguish between what is relevant and what is not. Humility is also a good quality for a beginning agent. As Knowles advises: "Be positive and don't be too proud to do menial tasks. Most importantly, find a mentor, get next to that person and learn from them."[22]

Agents also must be willing to follow general directives and procedures. This is an important way to minimize danger not only to agents but to the public as well. As D'Angelo explains, "[The ATF] has a bookshelf full of directives and manuals about procedures. If someone is sticking to the book, that minimizes the risk of something going wrong either administratively or tactically."[23]

Higher Education Required

While certain personal characteristics lead to success in the job, applicants must also meet education and experience requirements. Federal agents may be recent college graduates or may already have related experience, including as a police officer, in the military, or as a probation or parole officer. The FBI has more specialized degree requirements than the ATF. FBI applicants must qualify in one of four areas: law, which requires a law school degree; accounting, which requires an undergraduate degree in accounting or eligibility to take the CPA exam; language, which requires an undergraduate degree in any language and proficiency in a language the bureau needs; and diversified, which allows an applicant to qualify without these backgrounds, as long as they have a bachelor of arts or bachelor of science degree and three years of relevant work experience, or any advanced degree plus two years of relevant experience.

FBI trainees line up for target practice.

By contrast, although the ATF generally requires a bachelor's degree (unless the applicant has three years of qualifying experience), it does not insist on a specific course of study. Classes in criminal justice, accounting, justice administration, political science, forensic sciences, business, biology, and chemistry are helpful. However, according to D'Angelo, "ATF is more interested in how well you did than specifically what you did."[24]

Agents must be young. They may enter the ATF at age twenty-one and the FBI at age twenty-three. As a rule, an individual may not become an agent if he or she is over thirty-seven, and agents must retire at age fifty-seven, a testament to the physical demands of the job. After retirement, agents may start new careers, for example, as lawyers, or may work in security and loss-prevention for private companies. Of course, many other opportunities exist for men and women with the education and experience of these agents.

Rigorous Training Leads to a First Assignment

ATF agents undergo two training programs. The first ten-week session is held at the federal law enforcement training center in Glynco, Georgia. Prospective agents complete this training side by side with other federal agents, including those in the border

Training at Hogan's Alley

Law enforcement training is greatly enhanced by the staging of simulated crime situations at "Hogan's Alley," a "town" at the FBI academy in Quantico, Virginia. This excerpt from The FBI: A Comprehensive Reference Guide, *paints a vivid picture.*

To provide a realistic environment to train both new agents and local and state police attending the FBI National Academy, the FBI created a town setting called Hogan's Alley. . . . [It] includes a bank, post office, pharmacy, rooming house, bar/deli, pool hall, motel, trailer park, warehouse area, and a residential street that includes townhouses and apartments. . . . The town's pawn shop is actually a front for a gambling casino. Some of the buildings are real, such as the restaurant, which is used as a classroom, while other buildings contain offices. However, some structures are simply false fronts or use optical illusions to make them appear to be real buildings. Furnishings for the residential buildings and the cars come largely from property either seized or forfeited through FBI and Drug Enforcement Administration investigations. Although the offices are not used in the crime-scene exercises, arrests, surveillances, and searches take place outside and around them. The people who actually work in the offices in Hogan's Alley help make it a realistic setting as they walk from building to building or drive their cars through the roads. . . . Townspeople are recruited from Quantico or nearby Triangle, Virginia, to act as criminals or hostages. Trainees use deactivated weapons.

A staged crime in the town setting called Hogan's Alley.

patrol and Department of Defense. According to D'Angelo, the first program stresses basic rules and laws relating to arrest as well as basic investigation skills and procedures. Agents also learn how to track the activities and conversations of criminal suspects through legal wiretaps or by surveillance, following and watching subjects. New Professional Training, the second program, is completed during the agent's first year of service. Agency-specific skills are taught, for example, the differences between various kinds of machine guns, as well as the agency's specific mission and policies.

FBI agents complete sixteen weeks of training at the FBI National Academy in Quantico, Virginia. One area covered is self-defense, which includes developing physical fitness and learning to handle firearms. Trainees also learn how to comply with the con-

Trainees learn how to handle firearms in the FBI National Academy at Quantico, Virginia.

stitutional provisions that govern the arrest and interrogation of suspects.

After completing the initial phase of training for the ATF and the course of study at the academy for the FBI, agents receive their first assignment. An ATF agent may be assigned to a big city where specialized groups work on gangs, gun trafficking, or arson, for example. An agent assigned to a smaller city is usually not specialized and works on a variety of cases. Moving to the geographical location of the assignment is required, and all applicants must sign a statement confirming their willingness to relocate.

Good Pay and a Chance to Grow

FBI and ATF agents earn good salaries for law enforcement personnel, with the exact amount based on government pay scales for all federal employees. Because agents work long hours, they are paid 25 percent more than employees at equivalent job levels. The Bureau of Labor Statistics reports that in 1999, beginning FBI agents earned about $43,000 a year, including this extra pay. In nonsupervisory positions, an FBI agent's salary can rise to $67,300. ATF agents start in the $30,000 range; the maximum for nonsupervisory positions is somewhat less than that of FBI agents. In addition, agents may receive a cost-of-living allowance as compensation for assignments to particular locations.

Advancement is generally to supervisory and executive positions and may ultimately mean employment at the Washington, D.C., headquarters. Supervisory and management positions include special agent in charge (the head of a field office) or squad supervisor (the person in charge of a particular squad within the field office). At their respective headquarters, supervisory special agents may act as assistant division directors. Supervisory positions pay in the $60,000 to $90,000 range.

Opportunities Change with the Times

Opportunities for skilled, dedicated agents in the FBI and ATF will increase in the twenty-first century, in part because of the terrorist attacks of September 11, 2001. ATF agents are in demand to investigate airline crash sites for evidence that a bomb—rather than mechanical failure or another accidental cause—led to the crash. FBI agents are shifting focus from collecting evidence of drug-related and white-collar crimes to preventing further attacks by terrorist groups including those held responsible for the September 11 attacks. Thus, there is a demand for agents with skills in languages such as Farsi and Arabic. The changes are expected to be significant, as *Los Angeles Times* columnist Ronald Brownstein explains:

> The terrorist threat is demanding sweeping changes in the culture of entrenched government organizations. Agencies such as the Border Patrol and the FBI are shifting from old priorities—[blocking drug traffic], chasing spies—to apprehending terrorists. At [an October 2001] news briefing, [Attorney General] John Ashcroft said the challenge is demanding an even more basic change in federal law enforcement agencies: A shift in attitude from slowly assembling enough information

FBI agents stand at Ground Zero after the World Trade Center attack. Fighting terrorism is now a priority for the FBI.

A New High-Tech Facility

In December 2000, the ATF broke ground in Beltsville, Maryland, outside Washington, D.C., for a new facility for its National Laboratory Center (NLC). In addition to the NLC, which will move from Rockville, Maryland, ATF runs regional labs in Atlanta, Georgia, and San Francisco, California. Washington Post reporter Yuki Noguchi describes the state-of-the-art tools available at the new lab in "ATF Building High-Tech Lab; Beltsville Site to House New Investigative Tools."

As part of the [first] fire scene re-creation lab ATF will add hooded cells [at the new location] . . . to calculate burn rates on vehicles and multiple-story buildings. The building will be equipped with an extensive extinguishing system, sprinklers, water nozzles and a staff of trained professionals to deal with the fires. Among the lab's other new gee-whiz capabilities: a gas chromatograph that can identify how shards from a window or charred bits of furniture burned, a type of fire research software that helps in arson investigations.

to build a prosecution toward rapidly disseminating information to prevent future attacks.[25]

FBI agents who can detect and prosecute so-called cybercrime—crime committed using computers or over the Internet—will also be in demand in the twenty-first century. These crimes are expected to become more prevalent, but the agency has trouble hiring and keeping "cybersleuths" because these computer experts can earn more money in the private sector. A 2000 *USA Today* article quotes Stephen Schmidt of the FBI's technology unit, who describes the bureau's efforts to stay competitive: "Our pitch [to job candidates] is, 'We'll hire and train you if you stay for five years.' . . . The reality is we can't always keep them."[26]

While computer crime and terrorism are expected to preoccupy federal law enforcement agencies for the foreseeable future, it is impossible to predict how developments in the world and American society will influence specific priorities in the twenty-first century. However, the demand for well-educated, highly motivated individuals to fill these jobs should remain high.

Chapter 2

Correctional Officers

Correctional officers protect both prisoners and the public, in jobs that put them, perhaps more than any other law enforcement agent, in close, extended contact with society's offenders. "[The correctional officer's] first job is to provide for the public safety of the community [by preventing inmates' escape]. Next, we provide care and safety for whoever is sent to us,"[27] explains Eric Seleznow, public information officer for the Montgomery County (Maryland) Department of Correction and Rehabilitation. The correctional officer or corrections officer (CO) fulfills these responsibilities through a series of daily routines that range from checking cells for signs of tampering to keeping a special watch over inmates who exhibit behavior that suggests suicidal tendencies. These guard duties are carried out in a number of different settings, including prisons—state, federal, or privately run institutions that house criminals convicted of the most serious crimes. Officers also work in jails, locally run facilities that house newly arrested individuals and those convicted of less serious crimes. Correctional officers may also supervise inmates who have been sentenced to "work release," which means the offenders hold jobs and live in a designated facility in the community, and must follow strict rules about returning to the facility after work.

Preventing Escape

Correctional officers use a number of different techniques to prevent prisoner escape. In one routine task, guards walk the facility and inspect bars, doors, and windows for signs of natural wear and tear. Correctional officers are also alert to signs of tampering, such as scratches, which might warn that inmates are planning an escape attempt. In addition, COs search prisoners and any vehicles and containers brought onto the prison grounds for prohibited materials such as drugs or sharp objects that could be used as weapons.

Other security measures vary, depending on the level of security in force in an institution. For example, when handling the most dangerous prisoners, COs watch over inmates from control centers that contain closed-circuit television sets and computers to track prisoner movements. These guards have little personal contact with prisoners except when they transport them from their cells to daily activities that take place in alternate locations—for example, to the prison infirmary, where medical personnel provide basic health care. Guards may also transport prisoners to other locations, for instance, to an area inside or outside the prison building (but on the prison grounds) where inmates exercise. To guard the most dangerous inmates, COs may lock on

Female prisoners in jail uniforms relax in their cell.

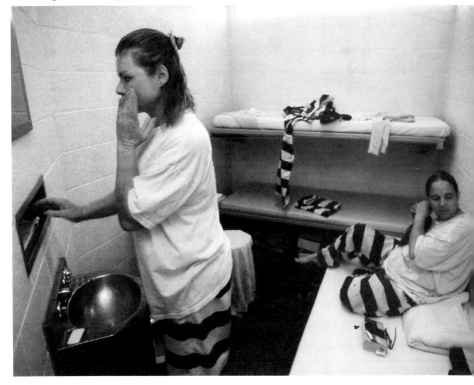

handcuffs or leg irons before allowing their charges to leave their cells.

Transportation may be necessary to locations outside of the correctional facility. One typical destination is an inmate's court hearing or trial. Preventing injury and escape during these outings, which usually employ buses outfitted with secure doors and windows, can be a challenge. That difficulty is summarized by *New York Times* journalist Tina Kelley:

Correctional officers handcuff an inmate before a search.

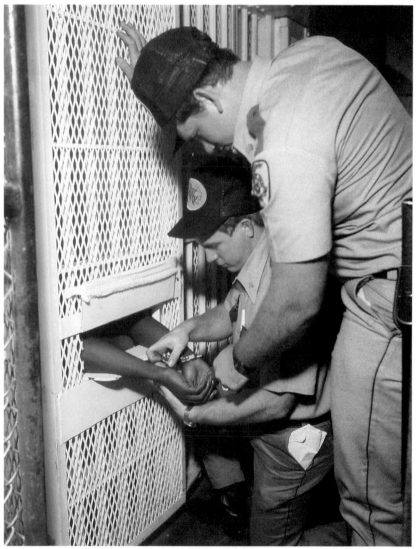

Because eating utensils can also be used as weapons, guards must be especially vigilant in the mess hall, even with juvenile offenders.

In Los Angeles . . . the trip from jail to court hearings can be up to 80 miles each way and take several hours. Of the 2,000 prisoners moved every day, at least one will probably free himself while on the bus. . . . With only two officers—one of them a driver—with each busload of 30 to 50 prisoners, the results can be frightening: fights with other inmates, attacks on officers and escapes.[28]

"Powder Keg"

Ensuring prisoners' safety and security is just as challenging when guards transport inmates from one location to another within a prison facility. Routine destinations include common areas such as the dining hall, which is considered a most unsafe setting, not only because many inmates gather for meals, increasing the risk of conflict, but also because prisoners have eating utensils—potential weapons— in hand. *New York Times* reporter Ted Conover describes the danger this way: "Fights in prison mess halls are like sparks in a powder keg: officers know they can lead to full-scale riots unless they are quickly contained."[29]

Guards keep close watch on inmate kitchen staff.

Kitchens, too, are areas where guards must pay special attention because inmates working there have access to cooking tools. To prevent prisoners from spiriting away utensils to use as weapons, guards follow special procedures. One example is described in *Corrections: A Comprehensive View*, by Ira J. Silverman and Manuel Vega: "To control tools and implements such as knives, inmates [preparing food] are required to check these items out. When they are returned many facilities require they be placed back on a shadow board, which has an outline of each item so staff can tell if an item and what type of item is missing."[30]

Communication Skills

Force and procedure are not the only methods correctional officers use to maintain order. While security measures involving restraining bars and handcuffs will always be utilized in correctional facilities, guards are increasingly expected to use interpersonal skills to anticipate and defuse potentially dangerous situations. Chase Riveland, former director of corrections for Washington State, remarks that this shift from a traditional emphasis on force is key to controlling prison populations: "What has changed over the years from the historical image is that today a person really has to rely a lot on communication skills."[31] Interpersonal skills allow a correctional officer to understand how to handle each inmate. Instead of using physical force, he or she can find better ways of solving problems, for example, by counseling inmates who have disagreements.

Some correctional officers believe that inmates are more likely to obey orders given by people with whom they identify. These officers may therefore develop a habit of mimicking the speech and mannerisms of inmates. However, not all officers agree with this approach. Jane Sachs, supervisor of administration and training at the Montgomery County (Maryland) Department of Correction and Rehabilitation, says, "Some officers have told me that the only way they can get inmates to comply is to speak like they do and come from their 'world.' However, there usually is an officer in each of my classes who disagrees and says that respect works just as well, if not better."[32]

Sgt. Sarah Lehane, a corrections officer in a maximum security prison for men, agrees with the idea that gaining the respect of prisoners contributes to a guard's authority. For Lehane, experience is the main means by which an officer gains that all-important respect: "Seniority is everything, and inmates respect officers who've put in time—they'll pull stuff on a rookie they wouldn't with me."[33]

Direct Supervision

Communication and respect are especially important in newer jails that are designed so that guards interact directly with prisoners. In these so-called direct supervision jails, inmates live in "pods," or relatively small housing units, where all daily activities—dining, education, family visits, and recreation—take place. The guards, who

A guard and inmate interact in the open environment of one of the newer prisons.

are unarmed but carry pager-type devices to call for help in an emergency, work and interact continuously with prisoners. They talk about personal problems and listen to complaints. They also observe the way inmates relate to others.

Because of this close contact, if inmates have a dispute, guards can help resolve the issues by talking to those involved instead of resorting to force. This kind of jail is called "proactive" because guards who know the prisoners personally are thought to be in a better position to head off problems. As described on the website of the Orient Road Jail, a direct supervision facility in Hillsborough County, Florida, "Direct supervision enhances the interaction between deputies and inmates, reduces inmate violence and vandalism."[34]

Major Elaine White, division commander of the Orient Road Jail, believes that direct supervision offers benefits to officers and inmates that would not be available in a more traditional setting. She explains that proactive management allows officers to "communicate with [inmates] and treat them as human beings until their behavior dictates otherwise." For this reason, White believes that the best guards in these facilities have extroverted personalities: "You can't be a recluse because you will communicate with people all day long."[35]

Caring for Inmates

In both traditional and proactive facilities, officers contribute to the care of inmates in many ways, including arranging medical help when needed. Escorting inmates to the prison infirmary is a normal part of an officer's job because that area provides for all noncritical health needs, including dispensing nonprescription drugs such as aspirin.

Guards also keep an eye on inmates who appear to be experiencing mental strain or depression. In such cases they may recommend and arrange suicide watches, during which the inmate is observed closely and kept away from objects that could be used to cause personal harm. Because juveniles sentenced to adult facilities are at high risk for suicide, guards in these situations must be especially attentive. In a report in *Corrections Today*, Barry Glick and William Sturgeon explain the particular care correctional officers take in monitoring youthful offenders in adult prison:

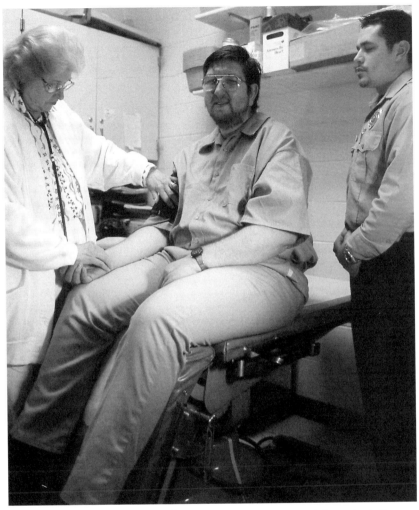

Part of a correctional officer's job is to escort inmates to and from the infirmary for medical exams.

Officers should know the habits of the inmates under their supervision and be alert for deviations from those behaviors. All youthful offender communications should be taken seriously, and no one should minimize the statements of youthful offenders. All staff should encourage adolescents to communicate freely and inform staff of suicide talk. Usually, this is a good indicator of what may come. Staff also routinely should observe for suicide-risk indicators and communicate their observation of potential suicide risk to other staff. . . . Staff should be alert to structural or other devices

One Source of Stress

While researchers study the causes of and remedies for correctional officer strain, one basic source of stress cannot be eliminated. Researcher Peter Finn summarizes the inherent difficulty of forcing others to stay behind bars in "Correctional Officer Stress: A Cause for Concern and Additional Help" from Federal Probation:

A fundamental feature of working in prisons and jails that causes stress is that people do not like being held against their will and being closely supervised. According to a researcher, "Any organization or social structure which consists of one group of people kept inside who do not want to be there and the other group who are there to make sure they stay in will be an organization under stress."

The confinement of prison is a constant source of stress for both prisoners and correctional officers.

that may be used to attempt suicide. It is critically important to provide timely assessment and treatment when suicide attempts are suspected.[36]

Severe Stress

Bearing the responsibility for the security and safety of the prison community can be a strain. In fact, as a group, correctional officers experience an exceptionally high level of job stress, which can lead to emotional problems such as burnout or depression. In addition, correctional officers have a higher than normal incidence of heart attacks, high blood pressure, ulcers, and other stress-related physical problems.

One of the most obvious sources of stress is the physical danger that these guards face. The presence of prison gangs, drug abusers, and predatory inmates raises the stakes for even the most experienced correctional officers. Journalist Ted Conover portrays Sgt. Sarah Lehane's brush with serious injury during a dining hall fight at a maximum security prison for men in Massachusetts:

> [Lehane] ran to the defense of a young officer who was down and getting kicked. After three minutes, the melee was over, and Lehane extricated herself from what she describes as "a pig pile." Nine officers had been injured, including her (a twisted knee and a banged-up shoulder); the one most badly hurt [suffered] a fractured skull and swelling of the brain.[37]

In addition to the danger of physical harm, guards may face health risks beyond stress-related ailments. For example, the population they deal with daily has a significantly higher than normal rate of AIDS infection. To protect themselves, guards follow procedures such as wearing latex gloves when contact is made with inmate blood.

Several additional factors cause stress for officers. For instance, guards may feel isolated because they work in buildings that are closed off from the normal routines of life. Instead of office coolers and desks, their surroundings feature bars, small windows, and communal showers. While correctional facilities vary in how comfortable they are for guards and prisoners based on their quality of

Correctional officers often feel isolated because they work in an environment cut off from the outside world.

design, age, degree of deterioration, and the skill of prison management, all share the distinction of being totally unlike the outside world. Eric Seleznow summarizes this reality: "It's like college dormitories. Some [institutions] are hell-holes, some are more therapeutic. The settings are varied and it's like nothing most people have seen."[38]

Guards experience what authors Silverman and Vega describe as an assault on the senses: "[Guards] may not even be able to hear themselves think because of the cacophony of sounds (doors clanging shut, the prison's loudspeakers blaring orders) that permeates many prisons. Added to this they may be bombarded by the mixed odors of urine, feces, disinfectant, sweat, and food."[39]

New guards—especially those who have never before visited a correctional facility—may be unnerved by this situation. Elaine White has seen more than one new correctional officer literally run from this distressing environment:

> I've seen people who arrive for the actual job after going through all the training and [then realize it is not for them]. They might be petrified of the inmates or feel too closed in. The first time they see someone buck-naked they might go out to lunch and never come back. . . . Anyone considering this career should tour a facility before they make a commitment.[40]

Other sources of stress include working odd shifts and overtime. Because inmates must be guarded twenty-four hours a day, officers work at night, either on a consistent or on a rotating basis. In a rotating shift, a guard works a few day shifts and a few night shifts with some days off. Guards quickly find the inconsistent sleep patterns disorienting. A CO who worked rotating shifts reports, "One day I pulled over to the side of the road because I couldn't remember whether I was going to work or going home."[41]

Researcher Peter Finn reports that some guards consider overtime a mixed but ultimately unwelcome blessing because the extra pay does not compensate for exhaustion and prolonged exposure to

---

A Chance to Help

In a 2001 conversation with the author, Chase Riveland, former director of corrections for Washington State, expressess his belief that jobs will be plentiful in the twenty-first century for people willing to work with others less fortunate:

[Careers for correctional officers] are expanding. This is also an era when there will be a number of retirements, so opportunities will be tremendous for those interested in interacting with a variety of people and being a role model for others who are less advantaged or who have serious problems.

a prison environment. As one interviewed officer says, "Overtime [OT] is great—I worked three OTs a week for 18 months. But I got burned out, and my supervisors didn't even acknowledge my contribution."[42] Finn notes a stress counselor's candid observation that these longer hours may create more stress for a corrections officer than someone in a more typical job: "Doing a double [shift] means spending 16 hours in a row with people who are not nice."[43]

Understaffing—having too few guards because of budgetary limitations or poor management—can also be frustrating and demoralizing for COs, who are expected to complete their daily tasks in spite of this problem. When one facility cut the number of guards in half, the remaining officers were expected to cover twice the number of inmates and twice the area. To Finn, one guard complained, "There isn't enough time for me to get inmates awakened, showered, and fed, keep my log books up to date, do my checks, and make sure the catwalks have all been cleaned and disinfected."[44]

Respect

A lack of respect for the correctional employee is yet another source of stress. Until the 1980s, COs were the least esteemed members of the law enforcement profession. As a group, they had minimal education and training, and standards for hiring were dismally low. In the last decades of the twentieth century, the quality and standing of those working in correctional facilities improved. Academy training became the norm and higher education was encouraged. In addition, the founding of professional associations such as the American Correctional Association and American Jail Association fostered an atmosphere of professionalism.

However, negative attitudes about COs still linger, both among the public and among officers themselves. Jane Sachs believes that the media play a role in painting a negative picture of correctional officers. For example, while police are celebrated for catching offenders, the public often looks down on COs as hardly more respectable than the offenders they spend hours guarding. Sachs also suggests that the media is quick to capitalize on more sensational situations, instead of celebrating when these professionals perform well: "[What about] the last movie you saw that showed corrections personnel as hardworking and dedicated? Miss that one . . . ? But you probably saw the one where the 'guard' beat up the inmate or took advantage of the inmate."[45]

Guards oversee prisoners working out. Prison workers are gaining more respect than they once had in the law enforcement community.

But Sachs believes officers share the blame for their low standing in the law enforcement community. Instead of taking pride in the challenging aspects of their jobs and sharing them with the community through career programs or while socializing, she finds individuals "who work in corrections who tell me they are not proud of their profession and often lie when asked what they do for a living."[46]

Order and a Chance to Help

While officers acknowledge these difficulties, many also find positive aspects to the profession. Seleznow is one who dispels the notion that because the milieu of a correctional facility is unusual, it is not a good place to work:

> It's not a pleasant environment, but it is a highly structured environment and a well-managed [facility] can be a decent place to work, [in fact] a much more reasonable place to work than people realize. [An officer may enjoy] acting as a role model, helping someone less advantaged through a difficult time, protecting inmates and the public, and working with other people an officer feels close to.[47]

Another positive aspect of these jobs is their paramilitary structure: Prison personnel wear uniforms and respond to commands from supervisors. Thus, employees have a sense of what is expected of them and what the routines of the day will be. They also share an equality that is beneficial to all officers, including women. As White points out, "Men and women are treated the same—same uniform, same pay, same assignments. Only bathrooms delineate who goes where."[48]

Better Trained but Still Underpaid

Conditions within prisons and jails are expected to continue to improve as education and training of guards improve. High school graduation or its equivalent is a minimum requirement in all states. However, higher education is an important plus for applicants in the twenty-first century because the field of corrections increasingly relies on communication and observation skills. As White puts it, the trend

A prison guard escorts female inmates. Job advancement for correctional employees depends on education and training.

toward hiring applicants with higher education is a positive one because it means having "individuals on board who are good thinkers, motivated, [and] articulate."[49] A college degree is a must for those who wish to advance to the highest supervisory levels.

White believes she benefited from a college degree in criminology because she understood the discipline of corrections going into her job. Other coursework that is helpful for correctional officers includes psychology and communications. Because guards handle increasingly complex security equipment and computers for tasks including e-mail and keeping logs, courses in computer technology are also useful.

Correctional officers must be at least eighteen to twenty-one years old, depending on the state. A clean criminal record, with no felony convictions, and U.S. citizenship are also required. Correctional officers must be physically fit, free of drug use, and must pass a written eligibility exam. Interviews, background investigations, or psychological profiling may be conducted on applicants.

The American Correctional Association and the American Jail Association have created guidelines for training of correctional personnel. Academy training lasts from four to twelve weeks. Two examples of courses offered are report writing and self-defense. Guards may pursue certification by professional organizations through examinations and additional training and experience.

In some areas the job still pays poorly. In 1999, beginning correctional officers' salaries varied from $14,600 in California to $34,100 in New Jersey. More experienced officers earn more—closer to $50,000 in the top ranges. Federal correctional officers started in the low $20,000 range in 1999.

Personal Growth

Correctional officers may advance through the ranks to supervisory, management, and executive positions. They may directly supervise the daily activities of other officers at the sergeant level. Or they may rise to higher levels, including, for example, major or captain, where they command the entire prison or specific parts or functions, such as the new-admissions area. At the highest levels they may have executive responsibility for a prison system, including its policies and procedures.

Despite opportunity for advancement, some officers work twenty years without seeking a change. However, others may move on to related fields, and their experience with inmates can be enormously beneficial in other law enforcement careers. As Seleznow explains, "[Correctional officer is] a law enforcement-related position, but also a counseling position. [The job] is an entryway into administration, police or investigative work, job counseling for offenders, juvenile counseling, drug counseling, or therapy, for example. For those interested in criminal justice or law careers, getting to know people who have spent time in jail is a good experience."[50]

Chapter 3

Police Officers and Detectives

Working together, police officers and detectives prevent, respond to, and solve crimes and help ordinary citizens during emergencies. Police carry out these duties through routine patrols that allow them to monitor activities within their "beat," or patrol area. They also respond to calls for help made to the "911" emergency phone line. They wear uniforms and work in shifts that provide community protection around the clock. Detectives, experienced officers with additional training, track suspects through investigative techniques that include interviewing witnesses and checking fingerprints taken from the crime scene. They dress in plain clothes and work nights and weekends when their cases require. Police and detectives may both be called upon to testify in court in criminal trials.

Traffic Duty

Regulating traffic is a key responsibility of police, usually in response to emergencies such as broken signals at busy intersections or auto accidents that block traffic. At the scene of an accident they also help calm those involved and call for medical help if needed. They make sure that evidence is preserved by taking witness statements and by measuring and diagramming the scene of the accident. They compile accident reports that include important details that might help prove in court which driver was at fault.

Although police respond to unexpected situations such as accidents, they also spend a significant amount of time on routine patrol.

By making their presence known in marked police cars, officers remind drivers to comply with speed limits and laws such as those requiring full stops at stop signs. These routine interactions with drivers are also important because they give police a chance to exhibit professionalism to the public. This is an important way to build trust that can lead to better compliance with police instructions. James J. Onder of the National Highway Traffic Safety Administration writes about this element of policing in *Police Chief* magazine:

> Officers' interaction with the driver during a stop will be a major determining factor in the driver's attitude toward law enforcement in the future. The goal is to achieve voluntary compliance with traffic regulations and acceptance of the laws and enforcement. People are more apt to accept a new or modified behavior if they trust and respect the authority. This is why professionalism is so important at the traffic stop.[51]

Traffic stops are also important because they are one way for officers to keep an eye on activity that could suggest or lead to crimes or other public safety risks. For example, an individual stopped for

An officer directs traffic on a busy street.

Officers on motorcycle patrol check a driver's identification during a traffic stop.

running a red light may be unable to produce a document showing that he or she owns the car. Police can cross-check a database of stolen vehicles and may find that the car is missing from its rightful owner. In another situation they may notice that a child is not strapped into a safety seat correctly.

Proving a Case

While police offer a first line of defense against crime, detectives focus on facts about crimes after an initial police response. For example, a car owner may place an urgent "911" call to say his or her car is being stolen. Police officers respond as quickly as possible to try to stop the criminal and to protect the owner and neighbors from any violence related to the theft. However, if the car and thief are gone by the time police arrive, detectives take over to try to recover the car and track down a suspect. Detectives question the owner for a description of the car and its license number. They attempt to get a good description of the suspect through interviews with the owner and any witnesses, for example, a neighbor out walking a dog who saw the thief in action. They use a special kit, police artist, or computer program to translate witness descriptions into a composite likeness. They compare the likeness with mug shots of known criminals or circulate the picture to other law enforcement personnel.

Once they track down a suspect, detectives attempt to obtain a confession. This phase of the detective's work takes patience, as Sergeant Louis Fata noted to *Kids Discover* reporter Linda Scher:

> When you question a suspect, you have to see if you can get evidence that can be used in court to prove his or her guilt. You need patience to question a suspect. Most people don't want to confess to a crime. But if you're patient, if you just take your time, if you have enough facts, people will admit what they have done. It may take you an hour, four hours, or three days, but in many cases, the suspect will want to talk and may, sooner or later, plead guilty.[52]

Specialization

Police officers and detectives in larger cities usually specialize in one class of crime. In a domestic violence unit, for example, detectives or police officers respond to calls from family members threatened with violence by other family members. Officers question the person lodging the complaint, the person accused of doing the harm, and any witnesses. They may arrest an abuser if they find a violation of the law. In one unit in Oceanside, California, a police department detective works with two assistants to provide follow-up help for victims of domestic violence, referring them to social agencies that provide assistance. They also reach out to educate the community. For example, in one effort, they collaborated with a local hospital, woman's center, and television station to produce a Spanish-language video on domestic violence.

The bomb squad is another specialized unit for officers who are willing to risk personal injury and who gain satisfaction from literal-

Risking Life and Limb

Working in a bomb unit is a challenging and dangerous assignment for specially trained police officers. Although they are taught to don bomb suits and bring in special equipment before handling suspicious materials, bomb specialists still risk being injured in emergency circumstances. Thus these specialists may suffer injuries to their limbs or hearing, even lose their lives, while protecting others.

ly defusing potentially dangerous situations under extreme stress. A member of the bomb squad is called to the scene if a suspicious object appears to be an explosive substance or device. The officer first determines if there is reason to worry by examining the object. If the specialist suspects an explosive, he or she dons a bomb suit and begins the harrowing task of defusing the bomb. Just wearing the protective gear is difficult. As journalist Lisa Vihos reports: "The suit is extremely heavy and very hot. A technician can only spend about 20 minutes inside the suit before another officer has to take over."[53]

Some officers may seek training to become K-9 officers. Police dogs have been used to aid investigations for centuries and remain one of the most valuable assets in fighting crime and protecting police personnel. Officers who elect to become K-9 experts are involved in the early training of their dogs. They become attached to the animals and may bring them into their homes to live. These officers often take their "partners" in as pets when the dogs retire.

Officers use dogs when they are searching for dangerous or illegal substances, from leaking gas to explosives to drugs, because dogs have an excellent sense of smell. Officers also rely on these dogs to provide protection. For example, a dog may rush a suspect who is armed and distract him long enough so that an officer may capture the criminal. However, this can result in the death of the dog, a sacrifice and loss that officers who work with dogs find difficult emotionally.

Police dogs are valuable assets in fighting crime and protecting police officers.

Police who work with dogs are called "handlers," and their role in the dog's training is critical, as portrayed by journalist Rick Boling in an article in *Animals* magazine:

> [The] future [police] handler . . . must create [a] special bond. . . . "Basically, for the first week or so, the handler does nothing but play with the dog, feed it, let it out, pet it," says [Skip Brewster, the national secretary for the U.S. Police Canine Association]. "In short, you make it rely on you for just about everything. The dog's drive will be based on how much loyalty you can create, how solid a bond you can establish. Once that bond is established, you basically have a friend for life."[54]

Officers may also become active in community policing, where they interact with adults and children in settings that foster trust and help citizens develop an understanding of how obeying laws increases security and safety. Schools are especially important connections for police officers because children are often quite receptive to police department messages. Police may become school resource officers, bringing cautionary messages about gangs and drugs into classrooms on a regular basis. Officer Willie M. Smith is one such officer who works in Miami-Dade County (Florida) public schools. He explains how using interactive activities, videos, and books helps him do his job: "Having such a selection of activities allows me to use the ones I feel best suit the needs of a particular group and gives them plenty of variety. The children get a lot of information that they may not even realize they're learning because it's taught in a really fun way."[55]

Police in smaller cities and rural areas may not develop specialties because specific crimes occur infrequently and because there are fewer officers to complete the work that needs to be done. In addition, officers who work in rural areas are more likely to focus on crimes that occur in homes between family members than on crimes committed in public by strangers.

A police officer teaches children about public safety with the aid of his dog.

Computer-ese Required

Police work is becoming more high tech in the twenty-first century, and officers typically use computers throughout their workday. For example, some patrol cars are outfitted with e-mail for communication with officers in other cars. In addition, officers use new software programs to add speed and precision to their work. For example, officers can use software developed by the National Center for Missing and Exploited Children (NCMEC) in Alexandria, Virginia, to quickly distribute alerts about missing children. The officer or detective investigating the case begins the process by interviewing parents to obtain a description of the child and the circumstances of the

Some patrol cars have built-in computers so patrol officers can send and receive information quickly.

child's disappearance. The investigator loads this information into the computer and scans a photo of the child that the computer converts into a poster. The investigator distributes it within his or her law enforcement agency so that other officers and detectives can help look for the child. The officer also uses the computer to distribute the picture instantaneously to the FBI and to other police departments.

Another software program that is becoming more widely used creates photographic likenesses of suspects based on eyewitness descriptions of facial features. Police have used composite likenesses for years, either calling in a forensic artist to make a drawing or using an "Identi-kit" to arrange, for instance, different types of eyes or noses on an outline of a face. An officer using the identification software works with a witness to pull up one of thousands of facial features provided on the database. The witness selects the characteristics and the officer uses the computer mouse to adjust their placement and the shape of the face. Even without special artistic skill, the officer can make a nose narrower or eyes wider. Journalist Bill Richards of the *Wall Street Journal* explains the program's use in a real case:

> [Lt. Mark Tulgetske, chief of detectives for the Jefferson County Sheriff's Department in suburban St. Louis,] says his detectives began using computers to generate suspect composites in 1996. Almost immediately, he says, they solved an armed robbery. The victim, a convenience-store clerk, provided a description of the robbers, and detectives passed on their photo composites to local TV stations, which showed them on the air.
>
> "We got calls right away," says Lt. Tulgetske. The callers identified one of the suspects, a 19-year-old man with a police record. "We pulled his mug shot and we said, 'Hey, that's him,'" the detective says. The man confessed and told police he recognized his own likeness from the composite shown on TV.[56]

Higher Expectations

In part because of the new demands of technology, police education expectations are rising and college coursework is a significant plus.

In fact, at the end of the twentieth century, nearly one-quarter of all police officers held college degrees, a significant change from 1970, when only 4 percent were college graduates. Degrees are often in law enforcement or criminal justice, but study is encouraged in other related areas, including government, business, psychology, physics, counseling, public relations, English, foreign language, and computer science.

The basic qualifications include high school graduation or its equivalent, U.S. citizenship, and possession of a valid driver's license. Any felony conviction disqualifies an individual. Applicants must pass a written entrance exam and polygraph and physical fitness tests. They may also undergo psychological and medical evaluations and extensive background investigations as part of the hiring process. Minimum age is typically twenty or twenty-one.

Preapplication experience can be helpful for candidates who aim to stand out. Courses or clubs that give experience in public speaking help develop communication skills. Volunteer experience in community policing not only demonstrates that a candidate is interested, but also gives a practical inside look at the career. Police in larger departments may be graduates of a cadet program in which high school graduates work as police clerks, with or without pay, while studying policing.

Some law enforcement personnel also believe that it is useful to have job experience that is unrelated to law enforcement. In the video *Becoming a Cop*, Costa Mesa (California) chief of police Dave Snowden enthuses about candidates with broad backgrounds because he believes they are better able to connect with people:

> Experience in other jobs, ranging from being a dishwasher to a gas station attendant to a salesperson . . . [gives] a broad perspective. . . . Those are the people you are going to be dealing with for the most part, people from the community, people that have all kinds of jobs, and the better understanding that you have of where they're coming from the better job you're going to do on the street.[57]

Academy Training and Pay

Once a candidate is accepted, he or she begins training at a police academy. Most academy programs last from fifteen to thirty weeks.

A police trainee learns the proper way to handle a weapon.

Here recruits learn about their specific agencies and how to write reports and comply with other administrative responsibilities. Many other skills are taught, including, for example, the proper and effective use of weapons. This includes not only firearms but also so-called intermediate weapons such as batons and pepper spray. To master these skills, recruits undertake shooting practice and test their skills in mock attack situations. Detectives receive their special training after gaining police experience. They learn more sophisticated methods of carrying out investigations, including how to handle and interview suspects. Each police specialty also includes training geared to the specific skills needed for those jobs.

The Bureau of Labor Statistics reports that in 1998 police officers earned less than $22,270 in the lowest pay ranges and over $63,530 in the highest ranges. Salaries increase as officers climb to higher ranks and to supervisory positions.

Staying Fit and Calm

While special training goes a long way toward making a good police officer or detective, these professionals must by nature possess or work to foster several important characteristics for success. Maintaining strength and agility is a lifetime commitment for these officers and detectives because being unfit can be dangerous for the officer, coworkers, and the public, especially since officers may confront younger criminals who have a natural fitness advantage. Therefore, officers should be physically fit to begin with and capable of committing themselves to a work-out program even before they begin their work in the field of law enforcement.

Police officers carry off a young activist at a gay rights protest.

Staying calm, no matter how an individual responds to police intervention, is another key quality for police officers. While a great deal of time is spent on routine tasks, police frequently encounter new situations involving people with unknown attitudes and unpredictable responses. This can be difficult because people sometimes get angry when police appear on the scene, whether in response to a heated family argument or a speeding car. Onder describes the personal discipline needed while on traffic duty: "Officers need to be courteous, balanced, and professional. . . . Officers should not be rude under the guise of officer control or officer safety. Also, officers should not respond to threats to their egos or get 'hung out on a limb' with nowhere to go except to escalate a disagreement. Being professional means possessing great skill to remain in control."[58]

Being calm and in control is also key to successfully testifying in court, an important part of a police officer's or detective's job. This can be especially difficult because of a heavy workload that makes remembering specific details difficult. Also, officers face defense attorneys who try to discredit police testimony. One California judge, William Bedsworth, describes these pressures in the video *Becoming a Cop,* and offers suggestions on how to deal with them:

> The police officer who testifies in court as a witness . . . is under attack from the moment he or she walks into the court room. . . . [He or she] is someone who has . . . perhaps been up for twenty-four to forty-eight hours straight, who now has to struggle into a courtroom, sit down on the witness stand and try to remember this one case of the hundreds he or she has worked on in the [last] year, and be an expert on it, remember all the details about it, stand up to cross examination about the case by a . . . lawyer . . . whose job is to make the police officer look bad. . . . [But] you have to be able to sit there and realize this person is [only] attacking [you] because [you are] the representative of the government.[59]

Facing life-threatening situations is a reality for police officers. In these instances, the consequences of not keeping calm and in control can be drastic, including personal injury or death to the officer

Work in law enforcement can be dangerous. Officers sometimes face life-threatening situations.

or others involved. Clearly, police work is not for everyone. Police officer Jim Wagner explains: "If you're getting into law enforcement you've got to realize that people are going to want to hurt you or even kill you just because you wear a badge. . . . You have to prepare for this possible event before you get into law enforcement. . . . You need to be able to handle pressure, handle fear, and be able to make quick decisions."[60]

A Real Risk of Harm

Even an officer who is psychologically prepared to deal with fear can lose his or her life in the line of duty. The frequency of officer deaths was described in the May 2001 "President's Message" in the *Police Chief*: "Last year 151 law enforcement officers were killed in the line of duty in the United States, representing a 13 percent increase over 1999. On average, a police officer is killed every 57 hours, making law enforcement America's most dangerous profession."[61]

California State Police Encourage Women

Working as a state trooper or highway patrol officer offers additional opportunities for those interested in policing. These professionals handle the law enforcement needs of a state, from patrolling its highways to protecting its governor. The California Highway Patrol (CHP) is an example of a state police agency. On its website, Captain Cathy Sulinski, a former track and field Olympian and first woman commander of the CHP academy, offers advice to women considering law enforcement careers:

Law enforcement is still considered by some to be a nontraditional career for women, but if you look at it, women have the skills

and attitudes to excel at this job. . . . We are excellent problem solvers and negotiators, [skills] which make up a large part of law enforcement. Some may think we don't have the physical capabilities for police work . . . but almost 10 percent of the 6,580 CHP officers are women, and our numbers are growing. The CHP's goal is to increase that number to 20 percent. And while women may voice concerns about dangers of law enforcement, our training teaches you to be safe on the job.

Women are becoming more visible in law enforcement.

An officer who physically survives an attack may have serious problems unrelated to any physical injuries. He or she may suffer post-traumatic stress disorder, which can seriously disrupt a person's ability to function in everyday life. One officer whose bulletproof vest allowed her to survive a gunshot to the chest recovered from the physical wounds in a few months. But she struggled with the emotional trauma for years. In an article in the *Police Chief*, Officer Marlene Loos describes the personal aftermath of the attack:

After I was discharged from the hospital, a misinformed psychologist told me "Don't worry, you're through the hard part, the rest of it is cake." Surviving the incident was instinct. Surviving the aftermath has been pure hell. It's been almost two and a half years since the shooting and every day is a challenge. I began suffering from allergies and night sweats as a stress reaction to my experience. Although my physical wounds healed in three months, I became hypervigilant and started to avoid confrontation. I began having recurring nightmares. Even after my attacker's trial in March 2000, the emotional challenges intensified.[62]

One of the rewarding aspects of law enforcement is interacting with members of the community.

Motivation to Help

In spite of its obvious challenges, police work can be a rewarding career. Officers and detectives report feeling fulfilled by aiding the public or seeing a criminal investigation through to successful prosecution. Good benefits and job security are also factors that make the job appealing. In addition, some officers, including those who are parents, find that working shifts outside of the typical nine-to-five day helps them manage their lifestyles in ways that suit them best. Other pluses include the opportunity to grow on the job, professionally and as individuals.

Perhaps one of the most satisfying parts of the job is the opportunity to connect with the community in a way that makes a real difference. Community police officer Willie E. Smith is gratified by the positive responses of former students, especially inner-city teens conditioned to respond negatively to law enforcement: "When I see them outside of school, even years later, they wave at me and say, 'Hey, Officer Smith! Do you remember me? You taught in my class a few years ago!'"[63]

Such positive interaction contributes to an officer's sense that he or she can make a real contribution to society.

Chapter 4

Criminalists and Crime Scene Technicians

Dramatic and suspenseful television depictions may confuse some people about the true nature of the job of gathering and analyzing crime evidence from a crime scene. But as Ronald Singer, crime laboratory director at the Tarrant County Medical Examiner's Office in Fort Worth, Texas, explains, "The major job [of crime scene technicians] is collection and preservation of evidence and reconstruction of a crime scene. They don't interview witnesses or do science [as they are sometimes portrayed on television]."[64] These tasks can be performed by specialized police officers but jobs are increasing for civilians with evidence-gathering skills who complete appropriate training.

The evidence and documentation gathered by technicians is analyzed and interpreted by forensic scientists called criminalists. Criminalists work in laboratories and must be skilled in the use of microscopes, other scientific instruments, and special chemical and physical methods that can help distinguish one substance from another, or tie blood or minute pieces of evidence to a suspect.

Collecting Evidence

At the scene of a crime, technicians gather physical evidence—objects and substances that can be analyzed by criminalists to provide important clues about a crime. Physical evidence is never the same from one crime scene to another. In fact, the possibilities are limitless, ranging from a murder weapon such as a knife or a gun to unique objects, for example, an ornate button. Physical evidence comes in all shapes and sizes, as authors Bruce L. Berg and John J. Horgan explain in *Criminal Investigation:* "In size, physical evidence may range from a battleship to a grain of pollen, from an apartment building to a sample of air."[65]

At the scene of a violent crime, technicians look carefully for signs of blood, one of the most valuable sources of information about what happened. Blood scraped from furniture or found on clothing can be analyzed in the laboratory to identify a suspect or victim. Technicians also look at how blood is distributed at the scene of a violent crime because this helps police and prosecutors reconstruct

Technicians search for evidence at the crime scene of a murder.

The Importance of Physical Evidence

Crime scene technicians gather objects and substances—physical evidence—from the scene that is crucial to proving guilt or innocence. In "Metal Detection: The Crime Scene's Best Kept Secret," from FBI Law Enforcement Bulletin, *author Richard K. Graham explains why this evidence can be more reliable and convincing to a jury than other types of evidence:*

Physical evidence reigns supreme over other investigative tools. Obviously, eyewitness accounts, as well as . . . victim statements, are important, but they can be influenced by external circumstances and even altered by outside pressures. Only physical evidence bears testimony that does not depend on memory . . . [cannot be intimidated,] and [is] unchanging. For this reason, no item of physical evidence, no matter how small, should be overlooked by the crime scene manager during an investigation. Often, fragments of physical evidence provide the only tangible strands that tie the [criminal] to the crime.

the crime step by step. For example, blood splattered on a wall in a room away from where a body was found may reveal where the victim first encountered a murderer.

Blood is generally easy to visually identify. However, technicians may have to search for objects that are not in plain sight. In these situations they use specialized equipment to locate objects that are not readily visible. The metal detector is an example of one such device.

Some metal detectors are sophisticated enough to distinguish between different types of unseen metals and can even be programmed to identify a certain object (a "target"). In one case a metal detection specialist was called to the crime scene to help find a bullet. The location of the bullet was critical to determining whether the officer or the suspect was telling the truth about where the officer was standing when the suspect shot him—a crucial fact since the suspect claimed that he had fired in self-defense. The technician first programmed the metal detector to specifically recognize a test bullet that matched the missing bullet. Then he proceeded with the search as described by Richard K. Graham in the *FBI Law Enforcement Bulletin:*

> Knowing the test bullet's [metal detector reading], the crime scene specialist initiated a systematic and exhaustive search in an effort to verify or discredit the officer's statement [about where shots had come from]. Metallic items unrelated to the shooting incident littered the search area. The operator ignored all metal signals until the detector located and reported a target item bearing the same characteristics as the test bullet.[66]

By finding that the bullet landed at a certain location, the technician helped prove that the officer's story was true.

At a crime scene, technicians use special care not to contaminate evidence that could then be ruled useless in investigating or prosecuting a crime. Therefore, when collecting or examining materials, technicians wear latex gloves and follow exacting procedures to lift, store, and label materials in bottles or plastic bags. This is important because they must be able to document the "chain of custody," meaning that they must be able to account for the continuous whereabouts of evidence from the time it is collected until it is presented in court.

These workers also follow safety procedures to avoid being contaminated or harmed by substances at the scene. They wear special gloves and clothing to protect them from chemicals or powders that might be harmful, or from germs and viruses such as HIV that are carried in human blood. They may also wear respirators if there is a risk that substances at the scene could cause cancer or create a biohazard.

Technicians also document the scene, taking careful notes that can be used by criminalists in their analyses and by prosecutors to develop a case. Even the smallest details are important as the technician completes this process. As authors Berg and Horgan explain, "It is not unusual for some seemingly unimportant item in the investigator's notes to become a pivotal point in the prosecution of the suspect."[67]

A Host of Specialties

Evidence collected by the technicians is carefully turned over to criminalists, who analyze it and prepare reports of their findings. Criminalists perform their work in laboratories equipped with scientific tools that include highly sophisticated instruments including, for example, microscopes. Because so many different types of evidence are examined, crime laboratories encompass a number of special scientific functions. For example, certain tools and scientific skills may be used to analyze drugs, while other methods and equipment are used to determine the identity of a

A criminalist analyzes evidence taken from a crime scene.

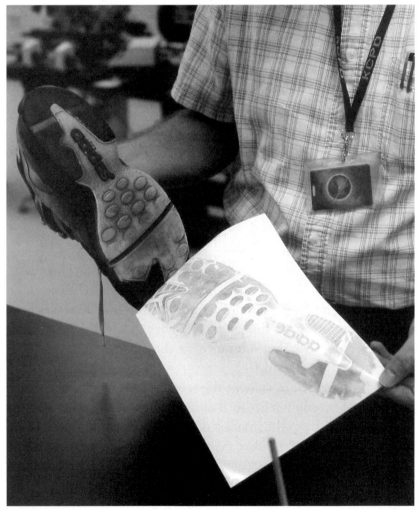

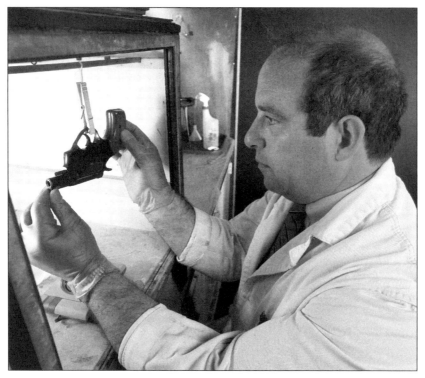

A criminalist tests a gun for fingerprints, one of many procedures used in solving crimes.

chemical. Thus, Berg and Horgan explain, "A crime laboratory is actually a large group of laboratories under one roof. Each laboratory specializes in its own area or branch of science. . . . Each laboratory, likewise, has its own specialized equipment, ranging from scanning electron microscopes to [other highly sophisticated equipment]."[68]

According to Singer, although some smaller laboratories or certain states employ criminalists with general skills, the trend is toward specialization. Singer reports, in fact, that generalization "is fast approaching extinction. Each field has become so specialized that to do more than one thing is becoming more difficult. Some [facilities] still have a generalist bent, [but in these] training could go on for ten years or more."[69]

Criminalists may, for example, specialize in the field of trace evidence. Experts in trace evidence use sophisticated microscopes and other instruments and methods to compare minute pieces of evidence brought in through the work of investigators and crime scene technicians. Criminalists may also be given a fleck of a substance that is not identified. To find out what this substance is, they take a known substance, for example, a chip of paint, and compare the two. They may also examine objects to try to find out what happened at the scene. These scientists can tell from a detailed examination of a broken glass just what occurred to break it, including the direction of a smashing blow.

A tiny piece of hair or a shred of clothing fiber collected at the scene can lead to identification of a suspect through comparison with samples taken from clothing of the suspect. Kelly Belcher, forensic trace analyst with the Tarrant County Medical Examiner's Office, explains how she examines evidence from clothing: "I scrape the clothing [and look at the particles] under a stereo microscope. Unlike a traditional school scope, the stereo microscope gives a three-dimensional image. It also has a longer working distance [so I can] look at larger or smaller objects." Clothing is not the only material that Belcher works with. New bits of trace evidence are constantly being brought in for analysis: "Trace analysis has a lot of variety. I come in and don't know what I'm going to get from day to day."[70]

Another specialty is in DNA analysis, a growing field that involves examining the DNA of suspects and comparing them with

A criminalist compares DNA found at a crime scene to the DNA of a suspect.

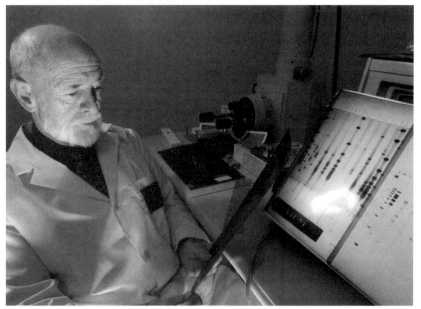

DNA Analysis Creates Need for Expert Criminalists

The importance of DNA evidence and of training criminalists in DNA technology is discussed by authors Robin S. Wilson, Lisa Forman, and Christopher H. Asplen in "Untangling the Helix: Law Enforcement and DNA," in Corrections Today:

The success of using DNA as criminal evidence can be felt across the country, by a rape victim whose perpetrator was convicted, or an investigator who closed a haunting 10-year-old murder case of a child. During the last 10 years, DNA technology has advanced so rapidly that many departments have found themselves without the proper training and technical assistance to maximize the value of this technology. Battles have shifted from proving the reliability and integrity of DNA as criminal evidence to how funding will be [provided] so officers can begin to use DNA in every capacity, not only as criminal evidence to convict a suspect, but as an investigative tool to identify suspects and link serial crimes. . . . [DNA] is an invaluable tool that will give officers the power to solve more crimes and offenders less opportunities to commit crimes again.

DNA collected at the scene. Because the DNA of each person (other than identical twins) is unique, a criminalist who extracts DNA from blood taken from the scene can compare it with DNA extracted from blood of a suspect. This method and its importance are explained by the authors of "Untangling the Helix: Law Enforcement and DNA," in *Corrections Today:*

Currently, the majority of criminal cases use DNA either to confirm or exclude a suspect as the source of evidence left at a crime scene. Because a person's DNA is the same in every cell, biological evidence from a crime scene can be compared to known samples from those involved in or suspected of a crime. Once a suspect is identified, a blood or cheek swab sample is collected and sent to the laboratory with the crime scene evidence for DNA analysis. The laboratory analyst compares the DNA profiles from the evidence and the suspect

A firearms specialist uses sophisticated equipment to determine how a weapon was used in a crime.

to determine if there is a match. Blood and semen are the traditional sources of DNA evidence, but law enforcement officers around the country are discovering that other evidence can be analyzed for DNA: . . . chewed tobacco or gum left behind at a murder scene, mucous on clothing or tissues, or skin cells left on the end of a weapon used to deliver forceful blows.[71]

Firearms specialists can reveal details about how weapons were used in a crime. In cases involving guns, they examine discharged bullets or shotgun shells to tie them to specific weapons that police or detectives have recovered from the scene or from the suspect. The criminalist also uses forensic techniques to reveal how the weapon was used. For example, if a shooting occurred in a bedroom, detectives want to place the victim and suspect in reconstructing the crime. A firearms expert can analyze physical evidence, for instance, a torn pillow, for signs that a bullet pierced it. The criminalist tests the fabric for signs of firearms residue at the tear. The criminalist also charts the path of a bullet by using mathematical calculations, including geometry.

"Sticklers for Detail" with Open Minds

This type of work requires precision from the moment a crime is discovered. Because technicians arrive soon after a crime is discovered, they have an intimate and immediate view of the event. Their observations are relied upon by other law enforcement and legal personnel at all stages of the investigation and prosecution of the crime. Therefore, in addition to exercising caution in handling the scene and evidence, investigators must be careful to avoid making hasty assumptions about what happened.

This open-mindedness is a required characteristic for investigators, not only because the rights of those involved are at stake, but also because making premature conclusions can obscure the true facts of a crime. For example, a knife found at the scene of a stabbing may or may not be the weapon used by the criminal. Until the object is analyzed for fingerprints, for instance, no conclusion can be made. For this reason, both crime scene technicians and criminalists must be what Belcher calls "stickler[s] for detail."[72]

A *firearms expert testifies at a trial.*

In the Courtroom

Careful, objective analysis is required of both criminalists and crime scene technicians because they may be required to report their conclusions in court. Testifying as a witness is one of the most important and difficult aspects of these jobs. Much of their findings is highly technical and must be explained in terms that laypeople, including members of a jury, can understand. A former chief of the California Department of Justice, Bureau of Forensic Services, describes the importance of professionalism when it comes to bringing one's evidence to court: "It is the duty of the forensic scientist to examine evidence in a highly skilled and eth-ical manner and to offer testimony that the prosecutor, court and the accused will recognize to be unbiased, incorruptible and enduring."[73] As an example of the importance of these personal characteristics, crime scene technicians who obtain certification from the International Association for Identification must adhere to a code of ethics that states, among other things, "I dedicate myself to serve mankind and to respect the constitutional rights of all people to liber-ty, equality, and justice. . . . I will never . . . permit personal feelings, prejudices, and animosities or friendships to influence my decisions."[74]

Where They Work and What They Earn

These important law enforcement functions are performed in a number of different settings. Crime scene technicians work for agencies, such as police. Criminalists work in a variety of locations. Singer estimates that there are about 450 laboratories across the country that employ a total of about 4,500 criminalists. Most crime labs are found within state, county, or city law enforcement departments, but some are established within the offices of a district attorney (prosecutor) or medical examiner (coroner). Federal agencies also have crime labs to ana-lyze evidence, and these jobs offer interesting opportunities for well-prepared candidates. The Federal Bureau of Investigation has the most extensive laboratory, but the Drug Enforcement Administration (DEA) and Bureau of Alcohol, Tobacco, and Firearms also have their own facilities. In addition, U.S. Customs has a labo-ratory to analyze smuggled materials. The U.S. Postal Service laboratory analyzes substances sent by mail, such as explosives, as well as fingerprints found on envelopes and packages.

Interesting jobs exist at the newer U.S. Fish and Wildlife Service labora-

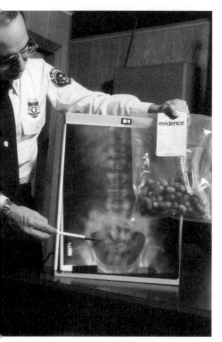

A U.S. Customs agent displays an X ray showing drugs hidden in a smuggler's stomach.

tory in Ashland, Oregon. There scientists support the agency's stated mission, which is "to conserve, protect and enhance fish, wildlife, and plants and their habitats for the continuing benefit of the American people."[75] Thus laboratory personnel are involved in examining wildlife remains to identify if a dead animal is a member of a protected species. They also match remains of animal victims with biological evidence linked to a person who might then be prosecuted for unlawfully killing a protected animal.

Criminalists earn between $20,000 and $40,000 in nonfederal jobs, with much higher earning potential after years of experience or upon becoming a laboratory director. Federal criminalist pay ranges up to $52,000. Crime scene technicians make less.

Degrees and on-the-Job Training

Education and special training are required wherever these law enforcement professionals work. An undergraduate degree is a minimum qualification for nearly all criminalist positions, and a master's degree is increasingly necessary for those who want to be competitive in complex fields such as DNA analysis or to advance to supervisory positions.

Criminalists generally have degrees in forensic science, chemistry, biology, physical anthropology, or physics. Study should also include mathematics, microscopy (the study of microscopes), statistics, and laboratory technique. Those who wish to specialize in certain areas may need additional training. For example, experts in determining the causes of criminal fires (arson) and explosions should also study electronics and building construction. Criminalists working with animal remains should prepare by taking courses in zoology and veterinary medicine.

Criminalists most often focus on areas linked to their academic major. For example, a chemistry major is likely to specialize in drug analysis, while a biology major may become a DNA analyst. Considerable additional education is acquired on the job, either through training or through self-study. Belcher, who is relatively new to her position, describes the typical educational activities of a young criminalist:

> I do a lot of reading. The interesting thing about this field is that there is always research to be done and new topics to be explored. It is important to stay current with the technology

Advice from Kelly Belcher

In an August 2001 interview with the author, Kelly Belcher, forensic trace analyst at the Tarrant County medical examiner's office in Fort Worth, Texas, gave this advice to students who are considering a crime lab career:

It all depends on what kind of subjects you like. Kids know what interests them and what they're good at. When you get to high school start taking classes in that direction. It's really important for kids to know that it's okay to like science, okay to be a science nerd. If science interests you, bring ideas for projects up to teachers. [Criminalistics] is a great field. There are so many different areas to go in to and there will always be a need for good, solid people with strong science backgrounds.

being used. A lot of reading is in journals, or in texts about instruments. Right now my focus is on hair analysis, so I am learning the characteristics of [that]. I will also go to the FBI training academy.[76]

For crime scene technicians, a high school degree is a minimum requirement. In addition, some agencies consider only applicants with college credit or degrees in science, forensics, or criminal justice. In some jurisdictions, technicians must be sworn police officers. Technicians receive hundreds of hours of training in many subjects including, for example, how to interpret the patterns of blood found at the scene and how to use specialized instruments such as metal detectors.

Dealing with Unpleasant Situations

Criminalists and crime scene technicians experience stresses common to the law enforcement field, including the fact that their services may be needed at any hour of the night or day. As Singer puts it: "We are generally on call 24/7 unless you can hide somewhere because major crime doesn't always happen during working hours."[77] Court deadlines and the understaffing of laboratories also contribute to job pressure. Because there is so much to do and so much responsibility associated with these jobs, some criminalists feel that they are underpaid.

In addition, these workers may work in difficult circumstances and be exposed to dangerous substances. For example, in the crime lab, some chemicals used to detect tiny traces of blood and other substances are known carcinogens and must be handled carefully. Blood handled by technicians and criminalists carries a risk of disease. In addition, crime scenes present other risks to technicians, who must work under any circumstance required. To get to a crime scene, they may have to move heavy objects out of the way. Or, work may take place outdoors in weather that is cold or rainy. If a body is found, for example, at the top of a beach cliff, a technician may have to make a difficult and dangerous climb to get to work.

The work of technicians may also cause mental strain because they may encounter the repugnant smells and grotesque or shocking sights associated with violent crimes. Criminalists and crime scene technicians must also deal with their own emotional reactions to crimes and the grief of the victim's family.

Coping and Serving

In spite of these challenges, criminalists and crime scene technicians find satisfaction in their work, part of which comes from learning how to deal with the stresses. For example, trace analyst Belcher described how she copes with death, a daily reality for anyone working in a coroner's or medical examiner's office:

> The best preparation [for taking evidence from bodies in the morgue is studying] anatomy and physiology in college. You have to look at the deceased individual as a specimen [and concentrate on looking] for things that are sometimes easily missed. It is very real and very tragic, but [your work] is the only opportunity to help find out what happened. You're doing it for the people who are still alive. I try to keep my life filled with other activities. I love music and sports and [enjoy those] and try not to take my work home with me.[78]

The bottom line for many criminalists is that they know they are fortunate to be using a science background in a field that is so central to the criminal justice system. As Singer puts it:

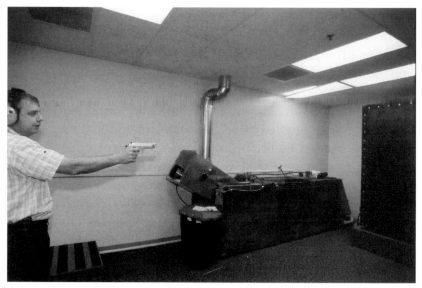

A forensics scientist fires a bullet into a rubber wall. The spent casing will be examined for comparison with casings from a crime scene.

The best thing about forensic science is serving the public and hopefully serving justice as well. We in the laboratory are just as happy to exonerate someone as to help convict someone. [I believe] if you last four years in this field you'll never do anything else. It's addictive being right here in the middle of everything, and using your [science] education in a way that few people get to do.[79]

Chapter 5

Probation and Parole Officers

Probation and parole officers (POs) participate in the administration of criminal punishment. They perform similar functions but in different settings. Probation officers initially help courts decide appropriate criminal punishment. One sentencing option includes probation, where the "probationer" is released into the community (instead of serving time in a correctional facility) under specific conditions. If probation is ordered by the court, the probation officer then supervises the probationer's compliance with these conditions. By contrast, parole officers assist parole boards in reviewing inmate requests for early release into the community on parole. Because parole is also granted with restrictions, parole officers, like

Members of a parole board review an inmate's request for early release.

probation officers, watch over parolees to make sure they obey the specific rules. Both probation and parole officers also serve as counselors to their clients (probationers and parolees), helping them find and keep work and adjust to living in society.

Assisting Parole Boards and Courts

In the role of advising courts on appropriate punishment (or, for parole officers, advising parole boards on release requests), a PO first conducts an investigation of the offender being sentenced or seeking parole. An officer begins the investigation by reviewing written material about an offender, including, for example, how the crime was committed and any past criminal conduct. However, much of the officer's time is spent conducting telephone or in-person interviews with the offender or with individuals who know the offender personally. For example, the probation officer is likely to talk with anyone who employed the offender or is familiar with the offender's personal lifestyle. This normally includes family members and acquaintances.

The officer asks questions about the offender's habits and behavior. Was the offender violent? Did the offender carry weapons? Did the offender interact with other criminals? How stable is the offender's family? A parole officer interviews prison personnel, too, to determine if the offender's behavior behind bars suggests a readiness to rejoin society or if, instead, the prisoner shows violent tendencies by, for example, starting prison fights. A parole officer also reviews the offender's plans to live outside prison to determine if they are realistic.

When the investigation is complete, the officer analyzes the collected information to predict the likelihood that the offender will commit another crime or otherwise be a danger if released into society. Based on this analysis, the officer prepares a report. The probation officer's report is made for the court and includes a recommendation for sentencing or punishment. For example, the officer may suggest time in prison, a rehabilitation program, or probation. The parole officer's report advises the parole board if release seems appropriate. Courts and parole boards rely heavily on the advice contained in the officers' reports and often follow it.

The Officer as Counselor

If probation or parole is granted, the officer assigned to the case begins the hard work of supervising the released client. Some of the work involved in this responsibility is conducted in the PO's office, where the officer begins to build knowledge about a specific client by compiling written information and by meeting with the client. Journalist Jennifer L. Harry reviews this initial phase in an article for *Corrections Today:*

> When [probation and parole officer Linda] Tabb is assigned a new offender, she conducts an interview in her office. Before the interview, Tabb must build a file from the information given her by the intake office. Along with the interview, she completes a social history, which stays permanently in the offender's file. Tabb goes over the rules of probation [with the probationer].[80]

Once the process is underway, officers make arrangements to meet regularly with clients; appointments are often held in the office. The offender is required to report at the arranged time and describe to the officer his or her activities and attitudes. During these meetings an officer acts in part as a counselor, helping the client with problems ranging from disagreements with family members to conflicts with a boss. Counseling also includes advice and coordination of housing for the offender and any treatment, for example, for

A paroled offender meets with his parole officer during one of many regularly scheduled visits.

drugs, ordered by the court. As Harry discovered in interviewing Tabb, establishing a good working relationship during these meetings is the key to success: "Tabb lets her probationers know that she and they are going to work through things together. 'With that attitude, you can get a lot of response from people,' [Tabb] says."[81]

Officers may carry out some of these counseling duties in group programs conducted at their offices or in meeting rooms elsewhere in the community. In such settings, officers meet with offenders regularly to work on improving their behavior and to teach them how to cope normally in society. Officers use a number of tools in group settings to encourage offenders' compliance with parole or probation conditions and to smooth their reentry into society. These tools

Coping After Prison

In a Georgia program, parole officers guide serious offenders through a course addressing four areas that officials believe help offenders make a successful return to society: decision-making skills, job training and employment, substance abuse, and education. This article, from the State of Georgia Board of Pardons and Paroles website, describes a gathering where offenders examine the consequences of selling drugs compared with the rewards of staying within the law:

[At the LaGrange parole office, housed in a former movie theater,] parole officers strapped with semi-automatic pistols buzz in and out of their small offices conducting drug screens, clicking entries into computers, or jangling car keys on their way to field rounds. . . . Ten men convicted of real-life, [unglamorous] escapades are gathered around a table, learning to correct the thinking patterns that led to their criminal behavior. . . . Today the LaGrange men are discussing "consequential thinking." . . . [Senior parole officer Barry] Davis asks the men to list the pros and cons of selling drugs, as well as the intensity of each of those factors. On the plus side are the obvious entries: status and power with a certain population, immediate access to the material world that seems remote otherwise. Under the negative column are what seem to be overriding factors: disappointing family, constant fear of prison or death.

include building trust and a positive sense of belonging, encouraging attendees with similar backgrounds to share concerns and successes, and showing the officer's personal interest in each client's success. In addition, officers work to help offenders change negative behaviors, many of which stem from a lack of careful thought about one's actions and their consequences. To accomplish this they may discuss offender problems and explore reasons for past criminal activities.

Officers also guide attendees through the steps to achieve positive change. In one Georgia-based program, for example, the goals are specially defined to include helping offenders reexamine their thinking patterns and motives, improve their education and jobs skills, and get and keep jobs. Senior parole officer Barry Davis describes the method as follows: "Parolees are usually impulse-driven. Through this course they learn to slow down and evaluate situations. When they practice these communication and decision-making techniques at home or work, they start building successes, and realize it's possible to dramatically improve their lives."[82] Community-Based Services director Beth Oxford, who is in charge of this and similar programs, illustrates the practical effect of the parole officers' efforts in these groups:

> Sometimes parolees in these classes will react in their old patterns, walking off the job from some perceived insult or breaking other technical parole violations, but they recover by using techniques they studied. Before the training, they would give up and keep heading down that road, like someone who blows an entire diet because they ate too much at one meal.[83]

Parole and probation officers regularly interact with other human services professionals to make sure that their clients get the support needed to remain stable in the community. Personal and job stability can help reduce the recidivism rate—the frequency with which prior offenders commit new crimes. In some states, however, such efforts may be more structured than in other states. For example, Georgia administers a program called Treatment and Aftercare for Probationers and Parolees (TAPP), in which officers work with other human services professionals to help released prisoners who are mentally ill or challenged. The officers enlist the aid of these social services employees to make sure that their clients can cope in society. The transition may be especially difficult for parolees who have been used to the structured housing, daily routine, and medical care of prison.

Parole officer Latasha Coley of the Georgia Board of Pardons and Paroles describes how she works with Ron Braswell, a TAPP social services coordinator: If they need a place to live, Ron finds it; if they need medication, he gets it; if they need transportation to an appointment, he's at their door to pick them up. If he notices something odd he'll ask me to stop by and see what I think about a situation, and I do the same with him."[84]

The Officer as Enforcer

The PO also acts at all times to enforce the conditions of release and to prevent new violations of criminal laws. To that end, POs use a number of techniques during meetings to determine if clients are telling the truth about activities and intentions. For example, in the case of an offender convicted of distributing child pornography, parole conditions likely state that the client cannot contact children, either in person, on the Internet, or by mail or phone. To make sure a client is in compliance with this condition, the officer may use psychological techniques to determine if a client is being honest about his activities. One officer reports firing a quick series of questions about what the client is thinking and has been doing. By not allowing the client time for calculated responses, the officer exposes inconsistencies. Another officer attempts to encourage her clients to reveal confidences by using a soft, nonthreatening tone of voice. Officers also watch the facial expressions and body language of clients to detect deceptive statements.

Field visits to the client's home or work yield important information about whether the client is behaving as he or she should. For instance, a curfew is sometimes a condition of release. To make sure the offender is complying, an officer may go to the client's house after curfew, even in the wee hours of the morning. Officers may also search a client's home and seize evidence that shows the client is not complying with release conditions.

Becoming involved with community policing efforts is another method officers use to make sure their clients remain law-abiding citizens. In these programs, parole or probation officers work in the neighborhoods where their clients live. They interact frequently with police patrolling the area, even accompanying the uniformed officers as they walk or drive their beats. This professional association allows parole and probation supervisors to observe community crime issues firsthand—for example, how an officer handles an arrest or keeps tabs on individuals in the community who might have information about ongoing criminal activity. In addition, through this contact, police officers learn the ins and outs of probation and parole systems, including, for example, how an officer interviews his clients to check on compliance with parole conditions.

Some experts believe that the clear association between policing and parole or probation supervision helps offenders realize that both are law enforcement functions, thereby positively influencing them to comply with the law and their release conditions. One program in Wilmington, Delaware, in which probation and parole officers patrol high-crime areas of the city late at night, has had a positive effect on the crime rate, as chronicled by journalist Harry: '[The program has] been rewarding,' [probation and parole officer Joseph] Paesani says.

Police and probation officers pair up to visit a parole violator.

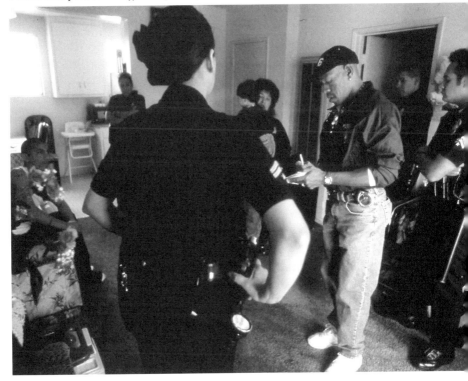

'We're having an impact on some of the violence in Wilmington.' Since the initiative began in June 1997, the rate of shootings in Wilmington has dropped significantly, Paesani says. 'We still have a ways to go, but we're heading in the right direction.'"[85]

Returning an Offender to a Correctional Institution

Another part of the role of enforcer is to initiate legal proceedings to return or sentence to imprisonment offenders who violate probation or parole conditions. Part of this duty includes exercising discretion to determine if a violation is significant enough to warrant this action. For example, an officer may overlook an offender's violation of curfew to buy a pint of ice cream because such behavior would not ordinarily pose a risk to the community. However, officers act swiftly if an offender's parole or probation violation can lead to public harm or the commission of a new crime. For instance, a typical parole condition for someone convicted of selling or using drugs is that he or she cannot associate with suspected drug dealers. The purpose of this condition is to make sure the offender does not participate in situations that can lead to renewed drug offenses. An officer who becomes aware of this type of violation would most likely initiate legal proceedings to discipline the offender or return a parolee (or sentence a probationer) to imprisonment. In a very few jurisdictions, parole officers have the power of arrest. In these instances the officers may wear bulletproof vests, work in teams, or enlist the assistance of police officers to protect themselves when taking a possibly violent offender into custody.

Officers may also be involved in investigations of new crimes. For example, if an officer is supervising a convicted arsonist and a suspicious fire breaks out near the offender's home, the officer questions the client to find out where he or she was at the time of the fire, and interviews witnesses and associates to attempt to verify the client's story. The officer may also study the files of several different clients to determine if past crimes fit the pattern of the new crime or if eyewitness descriptions of the suspect match present or past offender descriptions.

Stress from Many Factors

Significant psychological stress may affect some probation and parole officers, in part because their dual responsibilities of counseling and

A probation officer arrests a repeat offender. Repeat offenses are common.

enforcing often conflict. For example, the officer must constantly interact with clients but must not become emotionally involved in their problems. Another conflict is that the officer's mindset is to help the offender, but he or she must, above all, protect the public. Yet another dilemma is that counseling requires empathy and a show of sympathy but the officer also must be firm and authoritative to positively influence behavior and head off parole or probation violations and criminal activity. These inconsistencies may frustrate both the client and officer. As author Dean J. Champion explains in the book *Probation and Parole in the United States:* "In some instances, officers felt that their efforts in relating to offender-clients were frequently misunderstood and that they were perceived as antagonistic toward those they were supposed to help."[86]

Another source of psychological stress is the possibility that a parolee or probationer may commit a new crime, for which the officer may feel personally responsible, especially if a victim is seriously injured or killed. This is a very real problem because statistics show that many offenders do commit crimes again.

Working After Hours

Parole and probation officers may participate after hours in programs in the community. Officers may team with local police to visit high crime areas at night, when the most dangerous parolees and probationers are at risk of committing new crimes. By making their presence known in this way, parole and probation officers discourage illegal behavior.

The hard nature of the work is another source of stress. Officers are required to manage many cases at one time, and to be available when their clients are. Journalist Harry describes parole officer Linda Tabb's typical busy work schedule this way: "Tabb spends Mondays, Wednesdays and Fridays in the office and Tuesdays and Thursdays in the field. She also works two weekends a month to allow for visits with probationers who are not always at home on weekdays."[87]

Unpredictable problems may arise that require extra time on a single case or work outside of the usual forty-hour workweek. For example, if an officer believes a client is not following release conditions, surveillance of the client may be required to confirm activities. If a crime similar to a client's occurs, there is generally a great deal of urgency in trying to determine if the client was involved, through interviews with the client or associates or by a search of the client's home.

Parole and probation officers also risk physical harm at the hands of a client. This danger is a constant part of the job. Officers not only work in neighborhoods that are unsafe but interact daily with offenders, many of whom have served time or been convicted of serious, often violent crimes such as rape, robbery, assault, or murder. Even probationers, who are assumed to have committed less serious crimes because they are not serving time behind bars, can be dangerous because courts have been forced to react to overcrowding of correctional facilities by allowing probation even for individuals who have been convicted of crimes involving physical harm to their victims. As a State of California labor market brochure explains, "Probation and Parole Agents must work with upset, antagonistic, and/or manipulative offenders and their families."[88]

Optimism Required

Not only must officers be alert and physically prepared to protect themselves from harm, but they must have the ability and experience to evaluate the mental state of their clients. For example, they must be savvy enough to see beyond the obvious and to recognize patterns of thoughts and behaviors that might lead to parole or probation violations or criminal activity. One federal job announcement describes this skill as the "ability to discern deception and act accordingly."[89]

In all probation and parole positions, officers must be able to understand, interpret, and apply laws and legal documents, especially when reporting to a court or a parole board. Communication skills in this setting and in less formal discussions with attorneys, offenders, and the offender's family and associates are essential. Officers must be emotionally stable and fair-minded but firm in order to control and counsel clients and avoid being manipulated. They must

A parole officer counsels one of his parolees. Officers must be compassionate but firm with their clients.

also be self-sufficient in their daily work because they make decisions about how much time to devote to each case and when to act in response to a client's behavior.

Optimism is also required for these positions; to motivate positive change, officers must believe in an offender's ability to successfully improve his or her life. Officer Tabb describes the positive way she characterizes the probation program to her clients: "I always try to tell them it's a base for learning to do things better than what [they] were doing. A lot of people in the public don't know it, but people do turn their lives around."[90] A sincere interest in people and the community is also required for these positions. In praising Officer Paesani his supervisor said, "He is totally people-oriented, whether it's co-workers, offenders or the general public."[91]

A Social Science Field That Serves the Courts

Probation and parole officers work in agencies or as part of a court system at the local or state level. At the federal level, probation officers work as part of the federal court system. Because parole was eliminated for those convicted of federal crimes committed on or after November 1, 1987, work in the area of federal parole is limited. However, opportunities exist for federal probation officers throughout the country. Officers who excel may advance to supervisory positions or rise to manage agencies.

The jobs of parole and probation officer both require undergraduate college degrees at a minimum. A master's degree may be required to work at the state level. The undergraduate (bachelor's) degree may be in criminal justice, corrections, law, sociology, psychology, or related fields. Coursework in English and natural sciences is also recommended. Prior experience in counseling, corrections, social work, or human services may be required in some positions. Fluency in a second language is an important plus.

The expectations for federal officers are especially high. As with state-level employees, an officer must have a bachelor's degree, with federal job notices specifying criminology, psychology, sociology, criminal justice, human relations, business, or public administration as strongly recommended majors. Applicants with advanced degrees have an advantage over other candidates. In addition, the federal government requires that a candidate have at least one year of related experience, typically in state parole or probation offices. But can-

A parole officer reviews his caseload. His badge is visable in the foreground.

didates with high undergraduate grade-point averages or who have completed related graduate work or graduated from law school qualify without prior experience. Federal candidates are screened for drug use and must pass a thorough FBI background check, which is updated throughout the officer's federal career.

Training, including on-the-job, is provided, and may include courses in the psychological aspects of being a parole or probation officer. For example, POs may be taught how to control a conversation with clients. Because the job can be physically dangerous, POs also receive training in self-defense. For those officers who carry firearms, training in using them safely and effectively is also provided.

An Important Role and a Concern About Pay

Parole and probation officers play a critical role in the administration of American justice, as shown by the fact that they supervised more than 4 million parolees and probationers at the end of 2000.

Because prison populations and the instances of probation as punishment are expected to rise, prospects for employment are good. However, the number of jobs available will be affected by the levels of public funding for these positions.

Some officers believe that salaries for these jobs are low, considering the amount of responsibility and the number of hours officers typically work. Salaries range from about $26,000 to about $58,000 per year. More experienced officers and those with more education receive pay in the higher range. In 2001, federal pay ranged from $28,649 to $67,510.

Motivated to Help

Although they may struggle with a workload of dozens of active cases, and deal with challenging and manipulative clients, many of these officers ultimately feel that they are making an important contribution to society. And although the pay is often lower than they would like, officers express satisfaction at the level of individual responsibility and control they have over their workdays. For example, an officer determines when to schedule appointments and how to balance conflicting demands of clients by, for instance, devoting more time to an individual who appears to be struggling with adjusting to society.

Handling High-Profile Cases

Author Jennifer L. Harry interviewed parole and probation officer Linda Tabb about handling violent offenders in "Best in the Business: Helping Turn Lives Around," in Corrections Today:

"I don't have cases like [bad] checks, simple possession of marijuana or petty theft," says Linda Tabb, correctional probation specialist at the Clearwater, Fla., Probation and Parole Office. "I have the really high-profile cases, things that probably made the papers." . . . When asked if she's ever nervous or fearful dealing with such high-profile offenders, Tabb responds, "I've been with the state for almost 24 years and I've learned how to deal with people. Regardless of what the person has done, you treat them with respect. Then you can get that respect back."

Parole and probation officers are in a position to be positive role models and leaders for their clients. In fact, improving the life of a client is one of the rewards parole and probation officers experience. In the Georgia group program, for example, the officers' success was affirmed by one client who expressed his appreciation of the program by saying, "It's like there really is a light at the end of the tunnel."[92]

Notes

Introduction: An Array of Opportunities
1. Chuck Knowles, telephone interview with author, April 2001.

Chapter One: Federal Agents
2. Robert Hanley, "Federal Investigators Join Arson Inquiry in New Jersey," New York Times on the Web, September 2, 2000: http://nytimes.qpass.com/qpass-archives...00arc+db name=!db!+TemplateName=doc.tmpl.
3. Brad Garrett, telephone interview with author, April 2001.
4. Garrett, telephone interview.
5. Knowles, telephone interview.
6. Knowles, telephone interview.
7. Garrett, telephone interview.
8. Knowles, telephone interview.
9. John D'Angelo, telephone interview with author, April 2001.
10. Knowles, telephone interview.
11. Knowles, telephone interview.
12. Knowles, telephone interview.
13. D'Angelo, telephone interview.
14 Tom Connolly, telephone interview with author, April 2001.
15. D'Angelo, telephone interview.
16. Knowles, telephone interview.
17. D'Angelo, telephone interview.
18. D'Angelo, telephone interview.
19. Garrett, telephone interview.
20. Connolly, telephone interview.
21. Knowles, telephone interview.
22. Knowles, telephone interview.
23. D'Angelo, telephone interview.

24. D'Angelo, telephone interview.

25. Ronald Brownstein, "Federal Agencies Rushing to Meet New Demands," *Los Angeles Times*, October 22, 2001, p. A3.

26. Quoted in Edward Iwata and Kevin Johnson, "Computer Crime Is Outpacing Cybercops," *USA Today*, February 21, 2000, p. 1A.

Chapter Two: Correctional Officers

27. Eric Seleznow, telephone interview with author, April 2001.

28. Tina Kelley, "Calling on Technology to Build a Better Handcuff," *New York Times*, September 3, 1998, p. G3.

29. Ted Conover, "Hard Time, Behind Bars with 1,000 Male Convicts," *New York Times Magazine*, September 9, 2001, p. 152

30. Ira J. Silverman and Manuel Vega, *Corrections: A Comprehensive View*. Minneapolis, MN: West, 1996, p. 431.

31. Chase Riveland, telephone interview with author, April 2001.

32. Jane Sachs, "Professional Development for Correctional Staff," *Corrections Today*, vol. 61, no. 7, December 1999, pp. 90+.

33. Quoted in Conover, "Hard Time, Behind Bars with 1,000 Male Convicts," p. 154.

34. Hillsborough County Sheriff's Office, "Jail Division 1," www.hcso.tampa.fl.us/Jail%20Information/jail1.htm.

35. Elaine White, telephone interview with author, April 2001.

36. Barry Glick and William Sturgeon, "Rising to the Challenge: Identifying and Meeting the Needs of Juvenile Offenders with Special Needs," *Corrections Today*, vol. 61, no. 2, April 1999, pp. 106+.

37. Conover, "Hard Time, Behind Bars with 1,000 Male Convicts," p. 152.

38. Seleznow, telephone interview.

39. Silverman and Vega, *Corrections*, p. 301.

40. White, telephone interview.

41. Quoted in Peter Finn, "Correctional Officer Stress: A Cause for Concern and Additional Help," *Federal Probation*, vol. 62, no. 2, December 1998, pp. 65+.

42. Quoted in Finn, "Correctional Officer Stress."

43. Quoted in Finn, "Correctional Officer Stress."

44. Quoted in Finn, "Correctional Officer Stress."

45. Sachs, "Professional Development for Correctional Staff."

46. Sachs, "Professional Development for Correctional Staff."

47. Seleznow, telephone interview.

48. White, telephone interview.

49. White, telephone interview.

50. Seleznow, telephone interview.

Chapter Three: Police Officers and Detectives

51. James J. Onder, "Tips for Conducting Professional Traffic Stops," *Police Chief*, July 2001, p. 26.

52. Quoted in Linda Scher, "Meet Detective Fata," *Kids Discover*, July 1999, pp. 14+.

53. Lisa Vihos, "Bombs Away!" *New Moon*, July/August 2000, pp. 8+.

54. Rick Boling, "A Cop's Best Friend," *Animals*, July/August 1998, pp. 33+.

55. Quoted in Anuja Mehta, "Officer Reaches the Inner Child from the Inner City," *Corrections Today*, vol. 62, no. 2, April 2000, pp. 184+.

56. Bill Richards, "Cops Nab Perps with Digitized Drawings and Databases," *Wall Street Journal*, January 28, 1998, p. B17.

57. Quoted in *Becoming a Cop*, Costa Mesa, CA: WARArts, 1998.

58. Onder, "Tips for Conducting Professional Traffic Stops," p. 26.

59. Quoted in *Becoming a Cop*.

60. Quoted in *Becoming a Cop*.

61. *Police Chief*, "The National Law Enforcement Officers Memorial," May 2001, p. 6.

62. Quoted in Anna Knight and Ron McBride, "In the Line of Duty, 2001 Survivor's Club Update," *Police Chief*, May 2001, p. 33.

63. Quoted in Mehta, "Officer Reaches the Inner Child from the Inner City," pp. 184+.

Chapter Four: Criminalists and Crime Scene Technicians

64. Ronald Singer, telephone interview with author, August 2001.

65. Bruce L. Berg and John J. Horgan, *Criminal Investigation*. New York: Glenco McGraw-Hill, 1998, p. 64.

66. Richard K. Graham, "Metal Detection: The Crime Scene's Best Kept Secret," *FBI Law Enforcement Bulletin*, vol. 64, February 1995, pp. 10+.

67. Berg and Horgan, *Criminal Investigation*, pp. 27–28.

68. Berg and Horgan, *Criminal Investigation*, p. 62.

69. Singer, telephone interview.

70. Kelly Belcher, telephone interview with author, August 2001.

71. Robin S. Wilson, Lisa Forman, and Christopher H. Asplen, "Untangling the Helix: Law Enforcement and DNA," *Corrections Today*, vol. 61, no. 3, June 1999, pp. 20+.

72. Belcher, telephone interview.

73. Quoted in California Criminalistic Institute Forensic Library, "General Criminalist Requirements," http://caag.state.ca.us/caldojvl/ccilibrary/genreqs.htm.

74. International Association for Identification, "Code of Ethics for Certified Crime Scene Personnel," www.theiai.org/certifications/crime_scene/ethics.html.

75. U.S. Fish and Wildlife Service, "Learning About Us," www.fws.gov/lrnus.html.

76. Belcher, telephone interview.

77. Singer, telephone interview.

78. Belcher, telephone interview.

79. Singer, telephone interview.

Chapter Five: Probation and Parole Officers

80. Jennifer L. Harry, "Best in the Business: Helping Turn Lives Around," *Corrections Today*, vol. 60, no. 3, June 1998, pp. 76+.

81. Harry, "Best in the Business: Helping Turn Lives Around," pp. 76+.

82. Quoted in State of Georgia Board of Pardons and Paroles, "Parolees Stay Crime-Free with New Thinking Patterns," www.pap.state.ga.us/cogskills_update.html.

83. Quoted in State of Georgia Board of Pardons and Paroles, "Parolees Stay Crime-Free with New Thinking Patterns."

84. State of Georgia Board of Pardons and Paroles, "Treatment and Aftercare for Probationers and Parolees (TAPP)," www.pap.state.ga.us/tapp.html.

85. Jennifer L. Harry, "Best in the Business: Commanding Safe Streets," *Corrections Today*, vol. 60, no. 5, August 1998, pp. 16+.

86. Dean J. Champion, *Probation and Parole in the United States*. Columbus, OH: Merrill, 1990, p. 278.

87. Harry, "Best in the Business: Helping Turn Lives Around," pp. 76+.

88. California Employment Development Department, "Probation and Parole Agents," www.calmis.cahwnet.gov/file/occguide/PROBOFF.HTM.

89. United States District Court Northern District of Ohio Probation Office, "Vacancy Announcement 01-03," www.uscourts.gov/employment/ohproboffcer-01-03.html.

90. Quoted in Harry, "Best in the Business: Helping Turn Lives Around," pp. 76+.

91. Quoted in Harry, "Best in the Business: Commanding Safe Streets," pp. 16+.

92. Quoted in State of Georgia Board of Pardons and Paroles, "Parolees Stay Crime-Free with New Thinking Patterns."

Organizations to Contact

American Academy of Forensic Sciences
410 North 21st St., Suite 203
Colorado Springs, CO 80904-2798
Phone: (719) 636-1100
Fax: (719) 636-1993
www.aafs.org

Professional organization of criminalists, physicians, lawyers, toxicologists, dentists, physical anthropologists, document examiners, engineers, psychiatrists, educators, and others active in forensic science and its related fields. Publishes the prestigious *Journal of Forensic Sciences* and organizes seminars and meetings to promote education and excellence.

American Correctional Association
4380 Forbes Blvd.
Lanham, MD 20706-4322
(800) 222-5646
www.corrections.com/aca

Founded in 1870 as the National Prison Association, this group provides more than twenty thousand members with education and networking opportunities. It also administers accreditation of facilities and certification of individuals in the field of corrections.

American Jail Association
2053 Day Rd., Suite 100
Hagerstown, MD 21740
Phone: (301) 790-3930
Fax: (301) 790-2941
www.corrections.com/aja

This organization provides training and networking for jail personnel as well as publishes *American Jails, Who's Who in Jail Management*, a resource directory.

American Probation and Parole Association
2760 Research Park Dr.
Lexington, KY 40511-8410

Phone: (859) 244-8203
Fax: (859) 244-8001
www.appa-net.org
e-mail: appa@csg.org

A professional organization of American and Canadian probation and parole officers, agencies, and related institutions. Provides advocacy, education, support, and standards of conduct.

International Association for Identification
2535 Pilot Knob Rd., Suite 117
Mendota Heights, MN 55120-1120
Phone: (651) 681-8566
Fax: (651) 681-8443
www.theiai.org
e-mail: iaisecty@aol.com

This association promotes education, professional development, and research for forensic professionals. It also administers certification programs in forensic specialties as well as provides links to job openings.

National Association of Police Organizations, Inc.
750 First St., NE, Suite 920
Washington, DC 20002
Phone: (202) 842-4420
Fax: (202) 842-4396
www.napo.org
e-mail: napo@erols.com

An educational and advocacy partnership of police unions and associations.

United States Department of Justice
950 Pennsylvania Ave., NW
Washington, DC 20530-0001
Phone: (202) 353-1555
www.usdoj.gov
e-mail: AskDOJ@usdoj.gov

Makes available information about, and employment opportunities in, the FBI, DEA, border patrol, U.S. Marshals, and Federal Bureau of Prisons.

United States Department of the Treasury

1500 Pennsylvania Ave., NW
Washington, DC 20220
Phone: (202) 622-2000
Fax: (202) 622-6415
www.treas.gov

Makes available information about, and employment opportunities in, the ATF, U.S. Customs, and Secret Service.

For Further Reading

Books

Mary Price Lee, Richard S. Lee, and Carol Beam, *100 Best Careers in Crime Fighting*. New York: MacMillan, 1996. Useful summaries of career opportunities, including salaries, education requirements, biographies, and contacts.

Richard Saferstein, *Criminalistics: An Introduction to Forensic Science*. Upper Saddle River, NJ: Prentice-Hall, 1998. Technically comprehensive textbook, including a history of forensic science.

James D. Stinchcomb, *Opportunities in Law Enforcement and Criminal Justice Careers*. Lincolnwood, IL: VGM Career Horizons, 1997. Easy-to-read summaries, including contact lists, day-to-day work examples, and knowledge and skill expectations.

United States Department of Labor, *Occupational Outlook Handbook, 2002–2003*. Washington, DC: The Bureau: GPO, 2003. One of the primary sourcebooks for career information. Includes up-to-date summaries of more than two hundred careers, with information on job duties, outlook, required training and education, and salaries.

Periodicals

Charles W. Apps, "NCMEC Offers New Tools and Equipment to Law Enforcement," *Police Chief*, January 2001.

Hall Dillon, "Forensic Scientists: A Career in the Crime Lab," *Occupational Outlook Quarterly*, Fall 1999.

Websites

Bureau of Labor Statistics (http://stats.bls.gov). Comprehensive statistics on every aspect of federal employment, including jobs and wages. Includes a Kids' Page and link to online *Occupational Outlook Handbook*.

FirstGov (http://firstgov.gov). Official, all-inclusive gateway to U.S. government websites.

PoliceEmployment.com (www.policeemployment.com). A commercial website with job listings, links to law enforcement agencies, and tips on preparing and applying for law enforcement careers. Relevant pamphlets and videos are offered for sale.

United States Department of Justice, Kids' Page (www.usdoj.gov/ kidspage/kidspage.html). The department's research site for students. Contains easy-to-read material on forensic science, the FBI, and U.S. Marshals.

United States Department of Labor (www.dol.gov). The official website of the Department of Labor, containing links to volumes of information about careers. Link to online *Occupational Outlook Handbook*.

Works Consulted

Books

Bruce L. Berg and John J. Horgan, *Criminal Investigation*. New York: Glenco McGraw-Hill, 1998. Comprehensive, readable textbook on investigation, including review of specific crimes.

Dean J. Champion, *Probation and Parole in the United States*. Columbus, OH: Merrill, 1990. Detailed research study of the parole/probation system, process, and personnel.

Ira J. Silverman and Manuel Vega, *Corrections: A Comprehensive View*. Minneapolis, MN: West, 1996. A complete and detailed description of the field of corrections and the day-to-day work of corrections officers.

Athan G. Theoharis et al., eds., *The FBI: A Comprehensive Reference Guide*. New York: Checkmark, 2000. Fascinating look at the history, culture, and day-to-day life of the bureau.

Periodicals

Rick Boling, "A Cop's Best Friend," *Animals*, July/August 1998.

Ronald Brownstein, "Federal Agencies Rushing to Meet New Demands," *Los Angeles Times*, October 22, 2001.

Ted Conover, "Hard Time, Behind Bars with 1,000 Male Convicts," *New York Times Magazine*, September 9, 2001.

Peter Finn, "Correctional Officer Stress: A Cause for Concern and Additional Help," *Federal Probation*, vol. 62, no. 2, December 1998.

Carlienne Frisch et al., "Profiles of Four Occupations," *Careers and Colleges*, Spring 1996.

Barry Glick and William Sturgeon, "Rising to the Challenge: Identifying and Meeting the Needs of Juvenile Offenders with Special Needs," *Corrections Today*, vol. 61, no. 2, April 1999.

Richard K. Graham, "Metal Detection: The Crime Scene's Best Kept Secret," *FBI Law Enforcement Bulletin*, vol. 64, February 1995.

Jennifer L. Harry, "Best in the Business: Commanding Safe Streets," *Corrections Today*, vol. 60, no. 5, August 1998.

———, "Best in the Business: Helping Turn Lives Around," *Corrections Today*, vol. 60, no. 3, June 1998.

Edward Iwata and Kevin Johnson, "Computer Crime Is Outpacing Cybercops," USA Today, February 21, 2000.

Tina Kelley, "Calling on Technology to Build a Better Handcuff," New York Times, September 3, 1998.

Anna Knight and Ron McBride, "In the Line of Duty, 2001 Survivor's Club Update," Police Chief, May 2001.

Anuja Mehta, "Officer Reaches the Inner Child from the Inner City," Corrections Today, vol. 62, no. 2, April 2000.

Yuki Noguchi, "ATF Building High-Tech Lab: Beltsville Site to House New Investigative Tools," Washington Post, June 8, 2000.

James J. Onder, "Tips for Conducting Professional Traffic Stops," Police Chief, July 2001.

Police Chief, "The National Law Enforcement Officers Memorial," May 2001.

Bill Richards, "Cops Nab Perps with Digitized Drawings and Databases," Wall Street Journal, January 28, 1998.

Jane Sachs, "Professional Development for Correctional Staff," Corrections Today, vol. 61, no. 7, December 1999.

Linda Scher, "Meet Detective Fata," Kids Discover, July 1999.

Lisa Vihos, "Bombs Away!" New Moon, July/August 2000.

Robin S. Wilson, Lisa Forman, and Christopher H. Asplen, "Untangling the Helix: Law Enforcement and DNA," Corrections Today, vol. 61, no. 3, June 1999.

Internet Sources

American Academy of Forensic Sciences, "Criminalistics," www.aafs.org/employ/brochure1.htm#Criminalistics.

California Criminalistic Institute Forensic Library, "General Criminalist Requirements," http://caag.state.ca.us/caldojvl/ccilibrary/genreqs.htm.

California Employment Development Department, "Probation and Parole Agents," www.calmis.cahwnet.gov/file/occguide/PROBOFF.HTM.

California Highway Patrol, "Competitor to Commander: A Woman Pursues Her Dreams," www.chp.ca.gov/recruiting/html/new_academy_co.html.

Robert Hanley, "Federal Investigators Join Arson Inquiry in New Jersey," New York Times on the Web, September 2, 2000. http://nytimes.qpass.com/qpass-archives...00arc+dbname=!db!+TemplateName=doc.tmpl.

Hillsborough County Sheriff's Office, "Jail Division 1," www.hcso. tampa.fl.us/Jail%20Information/jail1.htm.

International Association for Identification, "Code of Ethics for Certified Crime Scene Personnel," www.theiai.org/certifications/crime_ scene/ethics.html.

State of Georgia Board of Pardons and Paroles, "Parolees Stay Crime-Free with New Thinking Patterns," www.pap.state.ga.us/cogskills_update. html.

———, "Treatment and Aftercare for Probationers and Parolees (TAPP)," www.pap.state.ga.us/tapp.html.

United States Department of Labor, Bureau of Labor Statistics, "Correctional Officers," http://stats.bls.gov/oco/ocos156.htm.

———, "Police and Detectives," http://stats.bls.gov/oco/ocos160.htm.

United States District Court Northern District of Ohio Probation Office, "Vacancy Announcement 01-03," www.uscourts.gov/employment/ ohproboffcer-01-03.html.

U.S. Fish and Wildlife Service, "Learning About Us," www.fws.gov/ lrnus.html.

Video

Becoming a Cop, Costa Mesa, CA: WARArts, 1998.

Index

accident reports, 45
accident scenes, 45
AIDS infections, 37
airline crash sites, 25
American Correctional
  Association, 40, 43
American Jail Association, 40,
  43
arson investigations, 11–13
Ashcroft, John, 26–27
ATF agents
  advancement opportunities
    for, 25
  application prerequisites, 22
  arson investigations by, 11–13
  communication skills of,
    20–21
  dangers faced by, 15–16
  earnings of, 25
  educational requirements, 22
  first assignments, 25
  independence of, 19
  initiative required of, 19
  job market for, 25–27
  job responsibilities, 11–13
  job satisfaction for, 17
  personal characteristics of, 16,
    19–21
  reputation of, 17–18
  specialization by, 19
  teamwork skills of, 19–20
  training for, 22, 24
  undercover work by, 13
  workload of, 16

beat (patrol area), 45, 83
Berg, Bruce L., 63

biohazards, 65
blood
  analyzing, 63–64
  diseases in, 65, 75
  DNA contained in, 70
bomb squad, 48–49
bomb suits, 49
bullets, analyzing, 64–65
Bureau of Alcohol, Tobacco,
  and Firearms (ATF), 11, 27,
  72
  see also ATF agents

cadet programs, 54
California Highway Patrol
  (CHP), 59
carcinogens, 65, 75
case agents, 13–14
chain of custody, 65
Champion, Dean J., 85
children, missing, 52–53
communication skills
  of ATF agents, 20–21
  of correctional officers, 9,
    32–34, 42–43
  of FBI agents, 20–21
  of federal agents, 20–21
  of police officers, 54
  of POs, 87–88
community policing
  by police officers, 50–51, 54
  by POs, 82–83
composites, 48, 53
computer crime, 27
computer skills, 52–53
confessions, obtaining, 48
Connolly, Tom, 18

contamination of evidence, 65
controversy, public, 16
correctional officers (CO)
  advancement opportunities
    for, 43–44
  application prerequisites, 43
  communication skills of, 9,
    32–34, 42–43
  dangers faced by, 37
  earnings of, 43
  educational requirements, 9,
    42–43
  health risks faced by, 37
  job market for, 39
  job responsibilities, 9, 28–37
  job satisfaction for, 41–42
  negativity of, 40–41
  stress felt by, 36, 37–41
  training for, 43
  work shifts of, 39–40
*Corrections: A Comprehensive
  View* (Silverman and Vega), 32
counseling duties, 78–82
crime laboratories, 66–67, 72
crime scene technicians
  clothing worn by, 65
  dangers faced by, 65, 75
  earnings of, 73
  educational requirements for,
    8–9, 74
  job responsibilities of, 62–65
  job satisfaction of, 75–76
  open-mindedness required of,
    71
  personal characteristics of,
    71–72
  precision required by, 71–72
  reports written by, 65
  stress felt by, 74–75
  training for, 74

Criminal Investigation (Berg and
  Horgan), 63
criminalists
  dangers faced by, 75
  earnings of, 73
  educational requirements for,
    73–74
  job responsibilities of, 8, 62,
    66–71
  job satisfaction of, 75–76
  open-mindedness required of,
    71
  precision required by, 71–72
  specializations of, 67–71
  stress felt by, 74–75
  workplace setting for, 72–73
curfews, 82
cybercrime, 27
cybersleuths, 27

day shifts, 39
depression
  of correctional officers, 37
  of prisoners, 34–37
details, attention to, 71
detectives
  dangers faced by, 57–58, 60
  job responsibilities of, 45,
    47–48, 57
  job satisfaction of, 61
  patience required by, 48
  personal characteristics of,
    56–58
  specializations of, 48–50
  stress felt by, 60
  training for, 55
  work shifts of, 61
dining halls, in prisons, 31
direct supervision jails, 33–34
DNA analysis experts, 68–70

dogs, police, 49–50
domestic violence unit, 48
Donnie Brasco (film), 13
Drug Enforcement
  Administration (DEA), 72

earnings. *See names of specific
  jobs*
educational requirements. *See
  names of specific jobs*
evidence
  at accident scenes, 45
  at crime scenes, 13–14, 62–65,
    70–71
  DNA, 68–70
  of firearms, 70–71
  importance of, 64
  trace, 67–68

FBI agents
  advancement opportunities
    for, 25
  application prerequisites, 17,
    21, 22
  case agents, 13–14
  communication skills of,
    20–21
  controversy faced by, 15–16
  dangers faced by, 15–16
  earnings of, 25
  educational requirements, 21
  first assignments, 25
  foreign language skills needed
    by, 21, 26
  independence of, 19
  information gathered by, 14–15
  initiative required of, 19
  job market for, 25–27
  job responsibilities, 9–10, 11,
    13–15, 17

job satisfaction for, 16–17
personal characteristics of, 16,
  19–21
reputation of, 17–18
specializing of, 19
teamwork skills of, 19–20
testimonies by, 18
training for, 23–25
undercover work by, 13
work experience requirements,
  17, 21
workload of, 15, 16, 17
FBI National Academy, 23, 24
federal agents, 11–27
  application prerequisites, 22
  communication skills of,
    20–21
  dangers faced by, 15–16
  independence of, 19
  initiative required of, 19
  job market for, 25–27
  job responsibilities, 9–10
  personal characteristics of,
    19–21
  reputation of, 17–18
  specializations of, 19
  teamwork skills of, 19–20
  see also ATF agents; FBI agents
Federal Bureau of Investigation
  (FBI), 11, 72
  see also FBI agents
federal parole work, 88
federal probation officers, 88–89
field visits, 82
firearms specialists, 70–71
fires, investigating, 11–13
foreign language skills, 21, 26,
  88
forensic scientists. *See* criminalists

Garrett, Brad, 13–14
group programs, for offenders, 80–81, 82
gun carriers, 13
guns, examinations of, 70–71
gun sales, illegal, 13

handlers, 50
HIV, in blood, 65
Hogan's Alley, 23
homicides, investigating, 13–14
Horgan, John J., 63
humility, 21

independence, in jobs, 19, 90
informants, 14–15
information gathering, 14–15
inmates. *See* prisoners
International Association for Identification, 72
interpersonal skills. *See* communication skills

job responsibilities. *See names of specific jobs*
juvenile inmates, 34–35, 37

K-9 officers, 49–50
kitchens, in prisons, 32

laboratories
  ATF, 27
  crime, 66–67, 72
language skills. *See* foreign language skills

medical care, for prisoners, 34–37
mental strain. *See* stress
mentally challenged offenders, 81–82

metal detectors, 64–65
murders, investigating, 13–14

National Center for Missing and Exploited Children (NCMEC), 52–53
National Laboratory Center (NLC), 27
New Professional Training, 24
night shifts, 39

open-mindedness, 21, 71
Orient Road Jail, 34
overtime, 39

parolee, 78
parole officers (POs)
  application prerequisites, 88–89
  communication skills of, 87–88
  community policing by, 82–83
  counseling duties of, 78–82
  dangers faced by, 86
  earnings of, 90
  educational requirements, 9, 88
  enforcing duties of, 82–84
  independence of, 90
  job market for, 89–90
  job responsibilities, 9, 77–84
  job satisfaction for, 90–91
  legal knowledge required by, 87
  optimism required by, 88
  returning offenders to prison, 84
  stress felt by, 84–86
  training for, 89
  workload of, 86
  workplace settings, 88

patience, for detective work, 48
patrol area, 45, 83
people skills. *See* communication skills
physical evidence. *See* evidence
physical fitness, 56
Pistone, Joseph D., 13
police academy, 54–55
police dogs, 49–50
police officers, 45–61
　application prerequisites, 54
　communication skills of, 54
　community policing by, 50–51
　computer skills of, 52–53
　dangers faced by, 57–58, 60
　earnings, 55
　educational requirements,
　　53–54
　interaction with POs, 82–83
　job responsibilities, 9–10,
　　45–47, 57
　job satisfaction of, 61
　personal characteristics, 56–58
　specializations of, 48–50
　stress felt by, 60
　training for, 54–55
　work shifts, 61
post-traumatic stress disorder, 60
prisoners
　AIDS-infected, 37
　in dining halls, 31–32
　in direct supervision jails,
　　33–34
　gaining respect from, 33–34
　medical care for, 34–37
　preventing escape of, 28–31
　transporting, 30–31
*Probation and Parole in the
United States* (Champion), 85
probation officers (POs)

application prerequisites,
　88–89
communication skills of,
　87–88
community policing by, 82–83
counseling duties of, 78–82
dangers faced by, 86
earnings of, 90
educational requirements, 9, 88
enforcing duties of, 82–84
independence of, 90
job market for, 89–90
job responsibilities, 9, 77–84
job satisfaction for, 90–91
legal knowledge required by, 87
optimism required by, 88
returning offenders to prison, 84
stress felt by, 84–86
training for, 89
workload of, 86
workplace settings, 88
probationer, 77
procedures
　for crime scene technicians,
　　65
　for federal agents, 21
　safety, 21, 65
profiles, victim, 13–14

recidivism rate, 81
relocation requirements, 25
repeat offenders, 81, 85
reports
　by crime scene technicians, 65
　by FBI agents, 15
　by police officers, 45
　by POs, 78
respect, for correctional officers,
　33–34, 40–41
respirators, 65

salesmanship skills, 21
Schmidt, Stephen, 27
school resource officers, 51
self-defense training, 89
shift work, 39–40
Silverman, Ira J., 32
special agents. *See* federal agents
specialization
  of criminalists, 67–71
  of federal agents, 19
  of police officers and detectives, 48–50
staffing problems, 40, 74–75
stress
  of correctional officers, 36, 37–41
  of crime scene technicians, 74–75
  of criminalists, 74–75
  of detectives, 60
  of police officers, 60
  of POs, 84–86
  of prisoners, 36
suicide watches, 34–35, 37

teamwork skills, 19–20
technicians. *See* crime scene technicians
terrorism, fighting, 26–27
testimonies
  by crime scene technicians, 71–72
  by criminalists, 71–72
  by detectives, 57
  by FBI agents, 18
  by police officers, 57
trace evidence, 67–68
traffic duty, 45
traffic stops, 45–47
training

  for ATF agents, 22, 24
  for correctional officers, 43
  for crime scene technicians, 74
  for detectives, 55
  for FBI agents, 23–25
  for police officers, 54–55
  for POs, 89
transporting prisoners, 30–31
Treatment and Aftercare for Probationers and Parolees (TAPP), 81–82

undercover work, 13
U.S. Customs, 72
U.S. Fish and Wildlife Service, 72–73
U.S. Postal Service, 72

Vega, Manuel, 32
victim profiles, 13–14
violations, parole (or probation), 84

Wallace, Barbara, 16, 17
weapons, investigating, 70–71
weapons, training for, 55, 89
wildlife, conserving, 73
witness descriptions
  at accident scenes, 45
  of crime suspects, 48, 53
witnesses, expert. *See* testimonies
women
  FBI careers for, 16, 17
  police officer careers for, 59
workload
  of ATF agents, 16
  of FBI agents, 15, 16, 17
  of POs, 86
workouts, physical, 56
work release, 28
work shifts, 39–40, 61

Picture Credits

About the Author

Patrice Cassedy, a former attorney, is the author of two other titles for Lucent Books: *Teen Pregnancy* and *Understanding Flowers for Algernon*. She has also published poetry and nonfiction articles, including interviews with book authors, filmmakers, and comedy writers. She spent a year in Washington, D.C., where she was able to contact and interview FBI and ATF agents to hear their career stories. Cassedy and her family enjoy travel, jazz music, and outdoor activities.